how to adopt a human

a cat's guide

written & illustrated by Bexy McFly

for Ollie,
who ~~adopted~~ rescued me

Hardie Grant

BOOKS

meet Percy

Oh, hi there!

My name is Percy, and I'll be your handsome guide throughout this book.

Adopting a human seems like a pretty big deal, huh? Well, you're not wrong. But there's no need to freak out just yet, because I'll be right here by your side every step of the way.

Stick with me and you'll be strutting into a forever home, living your best nine lives in no time!

The fact that you've picked up this book and have accepted your fate as a person-parent-to-be means the hardest part is over.* You're here, you're on your way! Look at you go!

Watch my butt carefully as I guide you through the beautiful and sometimes confusing journey of human adoption. In this book I'll help you choose your very own human and find the best one for you. I'll show you where to find them, what to name them, how to communicate with them, techniques for training them, how to discipline them and when to reward them!

You'll learn how adopting a human can build your confidence and make you a better cat – you'll go from scared shelter puss to confident kitty, commanding respect AND dinner in the same meow! Whaaaaat!!

If you have any questions or concerns along the way, just ask. Of course, I won't be able to hear you because that's not how books work, but I promise you'll always see an extremely pretty cat, one whose beauty will hopefully take your mind off whatever is bothering you.

Best fishes, Percy xox

*The hardest part is not over.

contents

part one

the adoption journey

page 4

part two

welcome home

page 22

part three

understanding your human

page 44

part four

human quirks & characteristics

page 62

part five

making your human the best they can be

page 88

part one
the adoption journey

why adopt a human?

Humans have been domesticated over the past few thousand years, almost definitely for the sole purpose of serving cats. They want and need to be taken in by us, as if it's some kind of primal necessity for them. If you think about it, we're actually doing them a favour even letting them near us.

If you want to live with someone who is whiny, needy and incapable of taking care of themselves, yeet this book and go adopt a dog. If you want an assistant who is relatively easy to train and produces actual results, adopt a human.*

Taking on the responsibility of a human is truly a win-win situation. The human gets a mentor who they can look up to (while looking down), and, in turn, a purpose for living. Meanwhile, you – their wonderful cat – will reap the many perks and rewards that come with a human, all with very little effort on your part.

Stuff like home ownership, unlimited grooming and nap time, predator-prey security, early hunting retirement, and the flexibility to set your own schedule could be your new normal. Pretty sweet, huh?

So, what's the catch? No catch. Not if you educate yourself and choose wisely, that is. That's where this book comes in.

Some say that humans don't come with an instruction manual. Well, this book is written proof that humans can be not only learnt but mastered. You don't need to be a pedigree Abyssinian to gain access to this kind of intel – you just have to be alive, somewhat coherent and willing to smell some questionable smells.

Check out the pamphlet below for a list of perks that come with the typical human adoption.

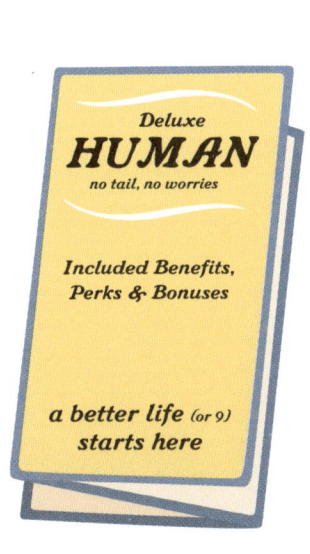

Deluxe HUMAN
no tail, no worries

Included Benefits, Perks & Bonuses

a better life (or 9) starts here

---

luxury⁺ accommodation

fancy collar with butler's bell

fully catered bowl service

complete litter service

slumber support

*subject to personal standards

---

special ^ guest appearances with optional meet & greets

24/7 entertainment & live comedy

unlimited respect and admiration

predator protection

^subject to tolerability

---

wellness programs
flea treatments
regular health checks
grooming service
bespoke petting
optional neck scritches

additional features
available with selected models

al fresco activities
excursions
treats on demand

---

*Results may vary depending on quality of adopted human.

the best time to adopt

Timing is everything when it comes to adoption. Instinctively, you'll be able to sense when a human is ready for you to come strutting in and take total control of their previously meaningless life. However, there may be circumstances where you are not afforded the luxury of readiness and you'll have to make your move quickly, with tactical precision. Still, trust your instincts – they will never steer you wrong.

The most common time to adopt a human is during kittenhood, as that's when you're cutest and most likely to be accepted by your first choice Ivy League human(s). As you get older, it becomes exponentially more challenging to meet your one and only, but rest assured that they are out there, waiting, and will never be out of paw's reach.

The most difficult time to adopt is when you're on your ninth life, you have three paws in the grave and your other paw is teetering on a slippery hairball. If you're a cat who has reached this point, congrats! You are a flea-carrying member of the elite FeSeS (Feline Senior Survivors) Collective, and you really can't afford to be picky about who you shack up with.

No pressure, but ideally you're looking for a really, really, REALLY good top-tier human who will groom you, love you, bring you treats and attend to your long list of needs, while expecting nothing in return. This will ensure you live in comfort and experience the benefits of human servitude as you await the sweet release of death (this also goes for cats who are not FeSeS affiliated).

Young, old or somewhere in between, do not doubt yourself or spiral into hopelessness. Your adoptee will come. You deserve this. You will be good at this. You will get your human, and they will be everything you ever dreamed they'd be, if not slightly underwhelming in the body hair department.

adoption vs rescue

There's a fair amount of confusion over what constitutes adoption vs rescue, but truthfully, the difference is negligible. Again, this all comes back to timing. Your instincts will lead you in the right direction, and most of the time that direction is a human in dire need of rescue, disguised as a perfectly normal-looking adoptee who appears to have their life together.

Many humans are not enlightened enough to know when they need saving, so some of them may resist (see 'so they're just not that into you', page 54). These ones can be annoying at first, but you'll never have any regrets.

who is adopting whom?

Would you believe most human adoptees actually think they choose who adopts them and when? Ha! Great job everyone, we fooled them. Bless those poor innocent doofuses and their bulky, underdeveloped brains.

Humans are quite egotistical, so they will often assume they know what they need. Some of the deluded ones will have a 'perfect' cat in mind who they've pictured being adopted by, and have looked forward to serving for eternity. The reality is they have no idea what's best for them and it's up to you to make them see the light.

A truly deserving adoptee human will be patient, just like you've been. They'll put their trust in the universe, sit back and let their adopter (you) choose them.

> Having doubts?
> If you've got cold feet, that's even more reason to adopt! Humans are excellent toe bean warmers!

LET'S GO SHOPPING!

there are many types of human available for adoption, but which one is right for you?

Choosing a human doesn't have to be arduous. You have good instincts – trust them. As cats, we were born with the natural ability to judge harshly, so all you have to do is put those skills to work.

Over the next few pages you'll find a handy breakdown of different kinds of humans on offer out there, and the pros and cons of each. This is not an exhaustive list, as humans come in many shapes, sizes and combinations. But it should give you a rough idea of what to look for.

Once you've made your choice, the tricky part is getting said human to take you home. If you're in a shelter, this can be particularly challenging, depending on your cuteness and charm.

If you're old, ugly, or missing some limbs/ears/random body parts, be advised that the person you adopt will have to be the very best kind of human.

If you are a shelter cat, you may wonder why you are in a cage. The cage is there to keep you safe as you are shown various humans to choose from. You'll notice these humans are free to wander around – this is so that you can observe them in their natural state and environment from the safety of your own private (or sometimes shared) fortress.

If you're outside in the world, one of the best ways to find a human is to wander around and try out different houses. You will know pretty much straight away whether you're adopting a nice old lady or a rambunctious family of ferals (those aren't the only two options, by the way). Make your way in. See if they feed you. Observe how they care for you and pay attention to you. Oh, and beware of stage five clingers.

You can read more about where to find a human on pages 12-13.

> Adoption is supposed to last forever, but ending up with a dud is a distinct possibility. You should certainly try your best to make it work, but if you're truly not satisfied you can always leg it and start again.

> It doesn't go the other way though – a human cannot simply un-adopt themselves ... I mean, why would they even want to?

couple

what?
a set of two humans who live together and may or may not share a bed

pros:
- double the food/love/attention
- double the laps to choose from
- susceptible to mind games (e.g. choosing a favourite is an easy way to mess with them).

cons:
- erratic feeding times
- sloppy schedule
- one of them will probably be way too into you
- may bring home annoying friends (or even a baby) at some point.

dog person

what?
an odd breed of human who worships dogs for unknown reasons, likely some sort of disorder

pros:
- dislikes cats and therefore already expects you to be a jerk to them
- fun to convert and remarkably easy to charm
- actually not horrible once you get to know them.

cons:
- has delusions of canine supremacy
- has no idea what a cat is or how to be owned by one (can also be a good thing)
- requires constant grooming
- may try to 'train' you, expect you to play fetch, or worse – wear a leash!

family

what?
a group of humans living together, usually comprised of at least one parent human (a), possibly one or more teen humans (b) and/or at least one small human (c)

pros:
- good selection of laps and beds to choose from
- always someone available to feed you
- always something happening.

cons:
- mo' people, mo' chaos
- you may be forgotten at mealtimes
- always something happening.

a. parent human

pros:
- most likely to feed you, care for you and scoop your poop
- quieter and better behaved than the rest.

cons:
- hard to sit on – is constantly getting up
- sighs a lot and talks to self (possibly insane or losing it).

b. teen human

pros:
- instant best-friend status
- lots of food scraps in bedroom
- easy to distract
- easy to embarrass
- homework to eat (not a cliché 'cos you're not a dog).

cons:
- may forget or refuse to clean up after you
- may become overwhelmed or bored with you, leaving you to seek out the default human of the house (parent human) for alternative care arrangements
- does weird things sometimes
- smells weird sometimes.

c. small human

pros:
- no regard for rules or dietary restrictions
- drops food constantly
- lower stature = easier to steal from
- will play with you (great news if you are still a kitten).

cons:
- mostly incomprehensible (can also be a good thing)
- may include you in strange rituals like wearing costumes and drinking tea* at a poorly manufactured table
- can be bossy, and rough with your ears and tail
- fingers are always sticky for some reason
- unpredictable limbs which are prone to flailing
- will play with you (not such great news if you are a self-respecting grown-up cat who values personal space).

*Tea does not actually exist. It's a big fat cup of lies is what it is.

senior human

what?
a human of advanced age, identifiable by wrinkled skin and slow-paced movement
NB The term 'senior' does not necessarily equate to 'highly skilled and knowledgeable'.

pros:
- several meals per day (won't remember whether or not you've been fed)
- sits down a lot
- endless supply of yarn.

cons:
- short life span, might die soon – leaving you alone, sent back to a shelter, or to inherit a less pleasant family member
- doesn't hear so well and therefore may be immune to incessant meowing
- smells weird
- uses talcum powder (don't inhale!).

emphatic feline enthusiast

what?
a human who has a true and justified appreciation of felines above all other species

pros:
- really knows their stuff
- will treat you like royalty
- will let you eat off their plate
- you can get away with murder.

cons:
- always home
- you'll probably have to share them with other cats (likely an unnaturally large clowder)
- will take photos of you constantly and share the embarrassing ones online without your consent
- will expect you to listen to their problems while they drink a lot of wine.

single human

what?
an independent human who lives alone

pros:
- full ownership – no need to share them
- undivided attention
- plenty of extra room in the bed
- you're (rightly) their top priority in life.

cons:
- may not have an actual life and spend too much time at home
- may go out too often and not adhere to your strict routines
- may bring home undesirables
- may come home smelling of strange things
- may tell you things you'd rather not know.

mix & match combo

what?
a group of humans you choose, who don't necessarily live together or know of each other's existence

pros:
- great for commitment-phobes or indecisives
- multiple dinner invitations per day
- boredom is a non-issue
- constant change of scenery – see the world.*

cons:
- only available to outdoor cats
- lack of consistency
- lack of accountability
- can be problematic if your humans find out about each other – you may be *gasp* presumed fed!
- if you get lost, or find yourself in trouble between humans, you're pretty much on your own.

*probably just the local neighbourhood

where to find a human

It's all well and good to get choosy about people, but where do you start looking? Check out this random assortment of places humans sometimes appear to be present. Your perfect human may be closer than you think!

in their homes

These humans are the most unsuspecting. Just walk in (if applicable) or stare through their windows to get a glimpse of what your new life may be like. Doing short stays in a human's house is a great way to test the waters before making a full commitment, but beware of crazies who try to trap you.

out and about

Fences and rooftops are great vantage points to spy on wild humans. They are more likely to do embarrassing things (like being their true selves) when they think nobody is watching. When the time is right, make yourself known. They'll feel seen, and you'll form a blackmail-based shame connection.

restaurant alleyways

The humans you find here are usually wearing all white, swearing a lot and OBSESSED with food (yay)! They are always stressed, so may or may not welcome your sweet affections. 9/10 will give you fish guts and other delicious morsels, but may not be open to full adoption.

office buildings

The probability of adopting a human here is very low. Humans in office buildings are always in a hurry, and they are too busy to do anything fun like get adopted by a cat. The only exception to this is a human who just got 'let go'. Despite being literally set free, they're sad and vulnerable. They also come with a stunning and spacious archive box.

shelters or cat cafes

The humans who frequent shelters and cat cafes are actively trying to get adopted. It's a little desperate really, but also kind of endearing. Shelters can be great for, well, shelter ... But you'll be surrounded by other cats who are equally keen on adopting, so the competition can be fierce.

schools

A school is a place filled to the brim with humans of the younger and smaller variety. Younger humans are the most open to being adopted, and are easily won over with soft smooches, a bit of cuteness and perhaps the odd trick or two.

All you have to do is choose one, follow them home, make your pupils huge when the bigger humans confront you, and the rest is just paperwork.

libraries or bookshops

While it's more likely you'll end up being a resident of the library/bookshop itself, this is a great place to meet humans. For some reason, the combination of books and cats is irresistible to the most intelligent ones who already live the ideal lifestyle you're looking for. Adopting a book lover means a lot of snuggle time and long periods of lap sitting.

by the seaside

Humans go nuts for the beach, yet they refuse to poop in the sand. They will actually submerge their whole bodies in the water (yes, really), splash around a bit, then come out empty-handed! Not a single fish! After that, they just sit around exposing their embarrassing hairless bodies! Weird.

Sure, lazing about in the sun is great, but the real seaside action is at the jetties and wharfs – anywhere near a boat. The humans here are fully clothed and may actually score a fish or two, though it's unlikely they'll share. Adopting a houseboat human is your best bet in this scenario.

what do you look for in a human?

Having trouble deciding? Try this quiz! — start here

Options:
- total capitulation
- a good comfy lap
- constant love and attention
- treats! All the treats!
- Just the essentials
- human? Pfft, I don't need no human

---

total capitulation → Do you want to sit on the same lap forever?
- yes → Do you want to be treated like a precious little baby?
  - obviously → Do you enjoy the company of other cats? — meow → **EMPHATIC FELINE ENTHUSIAST**
  - no → eww, gross → Have you ever eaten a bug on purpose? — who hasn't?
- no → (to "Would a noisy, chaotic household bother you?")

a good comfy lap → Do you bore easily?
- no → (lap forever branch)
- yes → Would a noisy, chaotic household bother you?
  - yes → Do you like human affection?
    - yes → Are you a biter? Be honest.
    - no → (to dog person path)
  - no → Are you averse to tail pulling and being touched with sticky dirty hands?
    - yes → Are you the jealous type?
      - no → **COUPLE**
      - yes → **EMPHATIC FELINE ENTHUSIAST**
    - no → Are you a biter? Be honest.
      - no → Can you commit to a long-term relationship?
      - yes → (dog person path)

constant love and attention → ... but only on your terms, right?
- yes → (to precious baby path)
- no → (to affection path)

treats! All the treats! → Would you sell your soul for just one more tasty morsel?
- yes → Do you have any self-control whatsoever?
  - yes → (to affection)
  - no → (dog person)
- no → (to essentials)

Just the essentials → Do you think love is essential to survival?
- yes → Ok, but ... what about neck scritches?
  - yes → (affection path)
  - no → Are you a biter?
- no → (wild path)

human? Pfft, I don't need no human → Could you survive on your own in the wild?
- no → (to neck scritches)
- yes → Are you sure about that, bro?
  - on second thought ... → (back)
  - did I stutter? → Do you have a decent amount of dignity and self-respect?
    - yes → Can you commit to a long-term relationship?
      - yes → **FAMILY**
      - no → **SINGLE HUMAN** / **SENIOR HUMAN**
    - no → Is learning tricks or people pleasing beneath you?
      - yes → (loop)
      - no → **DOG PERSON**

Results: EMPHATIC FELINE ENTHUSIAST • SINGLE HUMAN • SENIOR HUMAN • COUPLE • FAMILY • DOG PERSON

14

how to seal the deal

Adoption is a two-way street. And like most two-way streets, it can't be entered into without caution. If you bolt into this situation haphazardly, you could get flattened like a pancake and wind up in an early shoebox.

Finding the human(s) you want is only half the battle. There is still the matter of official adoption to take care of, i.e. getting them to agree to live with you.

Obviously, as a cat, you must be the key decision-maker, but it's probably worth considering the adoptee's wants and needs at some point too.

Anyone can fall in love, but if your chosen person walks right on by and doesn't even notice you, you could be headed for heartbreak.

There are several things you can do to seal the deal (see techniques for snagging your ideal human below), but remember not to sell yourself out. Consider your human carefully – they are a huge responsibility after all.

Alternatively, you may meet the odd human who desperately wants you to adopt them, but you're just not feeling it. In this instance, the best thing you can do is simply drive them away.

techniques for snagging your ideal human

✓ DO

- be cute
- feign affection
- smooch hard
- enlarge your pupils and stare intently (but not in a creepy way)
- headbutt human and/or rub yourself up against them
- expose your belly (but no touching! See page 103)
- make them feel like they're the only human in the world
- if you're separated by a cage: meow loudly, make eye contact, then reach a paw out through the bars and beckon them over with a sense of urgency (add a well-timed, pathetic meow to get them over the line).

✗ DON'T

- be gross
- cough until you vom
- growl/hiss/spray pee at them
- make yourself look diseased and unkempt
- scream in pain
- scratch yourself incessantly
- have a sneeze-a-thon
- feign a limp or tuck a leg up to look like an amputee (though some humans are suckers for disabled cats)
- keel over and stick your tongue out
- fake your own death.

ways your human may mark their territory

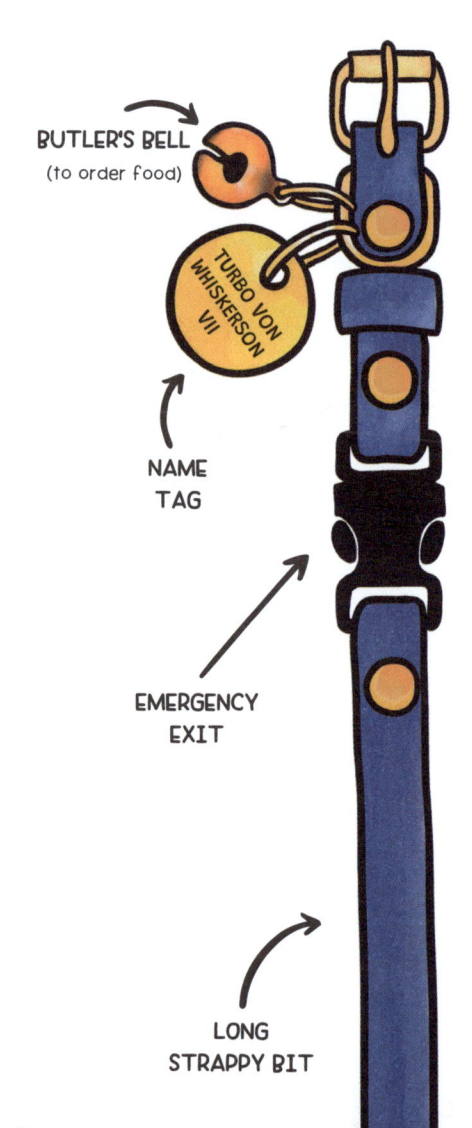

BUTLER'S BELL
(to order food)

NAME TAG
TURBO VON WHISKERSON VII

EMERGENCY EXIT

LONG STRAPPY BIT

the collar

Just as we like to name our humans, humans like to name their adoptees. This gives them a sense of responsibility and security, which is probably good for their development or something.

Humans may mark their territory by putting a collar on your neck with a tag featuring said name and a series of numbers. We're not sure what these numbers mean – perhaps a human code of some sort. Nobody cares, and it never comes up.

Basically, your collar is there to tell the world that a human depends on you, and you must be respected and revered as the overlord you are. You shouldn't take it off, no matter how tempting it may be to nude-neck it on the reg.

This collar will usually have a bell on it, which acts as a sort of butler's alert, presumably to alert your human of your coming so they can prepare food. This bell can be super annoying but you get used to it. If the bell is really causing you issues and you notice the butler function isn't working, you should be able to sever it with significant force and tenacity.

In some instances, your human may try to add flair to your collar by way of flamboyant accessories (see opposite). Whether or not you tolerate these is completely up to you. Take a look in the mirror. Do you feel fancy and pretty, or do you feel like a dork? Only you can decide.

GIRTH SCALE INDICATOR

some not-so-optional accessories

SHIRT COLLAR & TIE
(deceptively unprofessional)

CHARMS
(annoying, unnecessary)

PEARLS & DIAMONDS
(heavy, will dip into food bowl when you eat)

BOW
(uncomfortable but fancy)

POM-POMS
(not nearly as fun or delicious as they look)

BANDANA
(turns you into a big furry bad-ass, whether you like it or not)

the evolution of your name

creative licence

It is important to note that any name your human may give you will be for official business use only. They will usually refer to you by several variations of that name, some making no sense at all. The reasons for this include boredom, affection, endearment, and of course their unrelenting, narcissistic need for attention.

While name-reshaping can be confusing at first, it's worth noting that if your human starts morphing or changing your name, that's a clear sign they've accepted you as their adoptive caregiver.

One weird thing humans have a natural talent for is taking a perfectly good name and turning it into something perverse (or at times, downright offensive). The diagram on the opposite page shows an example of how they may manage to achieve this.

Be prepared to hear your name being called in a variety of pitches, tones and volumes. Pick one – preferably the most ridiculous and embarrassing one (for them) – and selectively respond to that.

There's nothing quite like being perched high on a tree in a compromising position while a panicked human is on the ground squealing, 'Yoo-hoo! Mr Squishy Bum-Bum! Come get your cuddle wuddles' in a glass-shattering falsetto, surrounded by onlookers.

Fortunately, no matter how many names your human saddles you with, it's not necessary to respond to any of them.

It can be concerning if you don't like what you're currently being called. The name you were initially given will likely go through a series of evolutionary phases before it sticks. In the example shown here, for a cat named **Ziggy Stardust**, it did not end well.

Ziggy Stardust thought he was safe with 'Ziggy' or 'Zig' for a really long time, until one day his human brought home some Jerk Store comedian. Before Ziggy knew it, he was being addressed as 'Pink Nips' and 'Sir Nipple'. Can you even imagine? Poor Sir Nipple.

Of course, this is an extreme scenario, which presumably won't happen to you. Surely not. Well, maybe. One-in-five chance, max.

How long each name lasts, and how detrimental it is to your dignity, depends on a number of factors such as catchiness, cleverness, cuteness and comedic value. Think to yourself: Do I embody the traits of the name I've been given? Maybe Ziggy Stardust really did act like a nipple, or maybe he showed them off a lot, and that's why it stuck. Did you ever think of that, Sir Nipple? Did you?

As demonstrated in this beautifully illustrated collar-tag timeline, your name can change dramatically over the course of your nine lives – and not necessarily for the better.

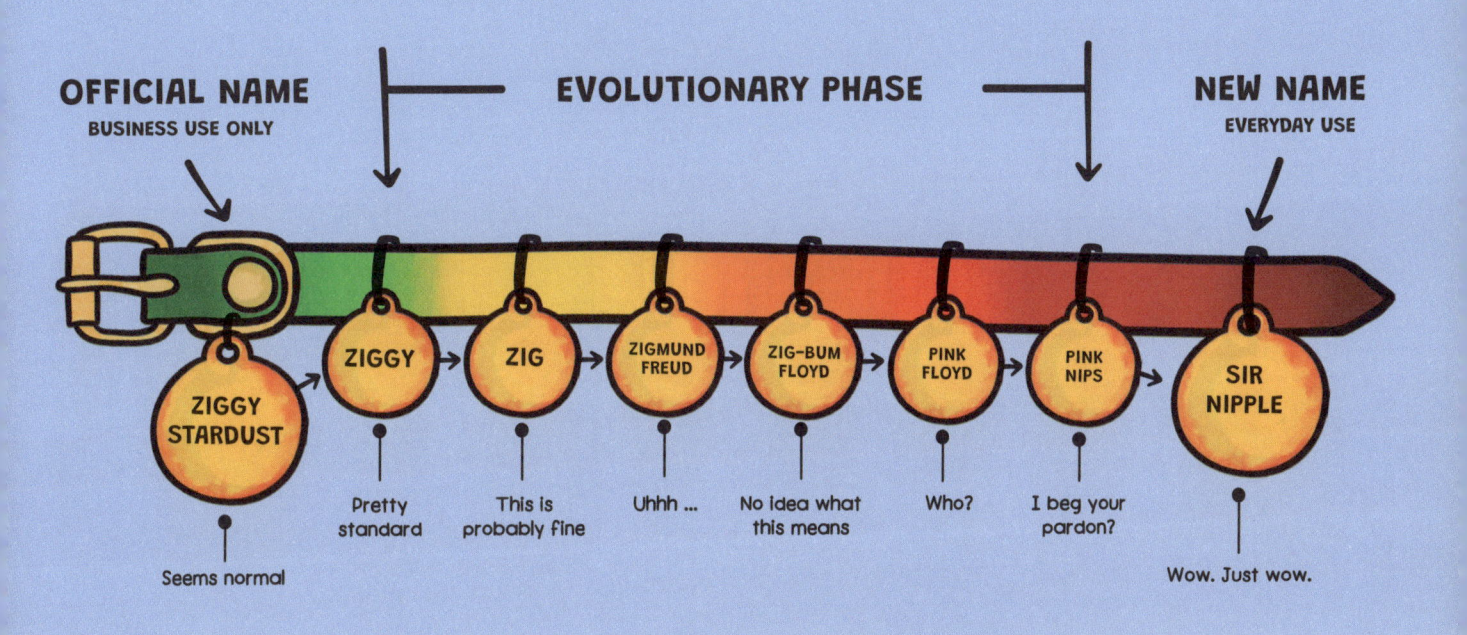

OFFICIAL NAME — BUSINESS USE ONLY: ZIGGY STARDUST (Seems normal)

EVOLUTIONARY PHASE:
- ZIGGY — Pretty standard
- ZIG — This is probably fine
- ZIGMUND FREUD — Uhhh …
- ZIG-BUM FLOYD — No idea what this means
- PINK FLOYD — Who?
- PINK NIPS — I beg your pardon?

NEW NAME — EVERYDAY USE: SIR NIPPLE (Wow. Just wow.)

singing

Humans cannot meow, though they certainly aren't afraid to try. Unfortunately, even their best attempts at meowing come out as gibberish. This is why some humans choose to sing – and no matter how terrible they sound, they will persist.

Your name will probably be your human's favourite word to sing, and you their favourite subject matter (can you blame them?), so try to be tolerant.

Believe it or not, singing is usually a sign of happiness in humans. Singing your name is very high praise, so you should feel special if your human makes up a jingle, a ballad or even a whole freaking album about you. It's an honour where they come from. Yes, seriously!

HOT TIP: If your human's singing escalates into dancing, avert your eyes – it's not worth the trauma. Then promptly escort yourself out of the room and stay hidden until all gyration subsides.

If it gets to the point where you need to solicit an emergency stop, simply begin to vomit.

naming your human

Humans usually come pre-named. However, those names are completely irrelevant and you don't need to bother learning or remembering them.

If you live with multiple humans and other cats, it can be useful to mentally label them so you can keep track of them, or simply for your own personal reference.

When choosing a name, try to go with something descriptive or easy to remember. Humans have a lot of fun identifying characteristics you can use to come up with something creative.

Just remember that the human brain isn't capable of processing the intricacies of feline communication – you can call a human anything you want and all they'll hear is 'Meow'. In fact, most humans probably think their name is 'Meow'. It must get very confusing for them, but that's really not your problem.

DID YOU KNOW?
There's not a single human on Earth who knows their real name! They're all just walking around telling people to call them, like ... Gary, or whatever.

HELLO!
MY NAME IS
Meow

most popular names for cat-adopted humans

- ⭐ Warmlap
- ⭐ Feeder
- ⭐ Biggie
- ⭐ Stinky
- ⭐ Biggie McStinky
- ⭐ Shoefoot
- ⭐ Buttwiper
- ⭐ Hairpatch
- ⭐ Jimmy Two-Legs
- ⭐ Shortclaw
- ⭐ Hind-Walker
- ⭐ Thumbledore
- ⭐ Spooner
- ⭐ Skinny Von No-Hair
- ⭐ Poopscooper
- ⭐ Mock Socks
- ⭐ Faux Paw
- ⭐ T.H.O.T. (That Human Over There)

starting forever off right
basic rules of paw

establish loyalty early on

Locate the main human (the one who feeds you and scoops your poop the most) and pledge your undying loyalty to them. It doesn't matter if this loyalty is completely disingenuous – it's in your best interest to be considered the golden child by this particular human for the rest of your nine lives. Sit near them, follow them around – whatever it takes!

set clear boundaries

If you're the kind of cat who doesn't like to be picked up, make that clear straight away. Of course, you reserve the right to change your mind later on, but it'll be a lot harder to train unwanted behaviours out of your human if you let them get away with them early on. Don't like people being all up in your face? Now's the time to start swiping.

you call the shots

It's important your human holds you in the highest regard and shows you nothing but respect at all times. You cannot afford to look weak or uncertain in front of them, especially in the beginning of your relationship, because they'll feel unsteady and start acting out. Conversely, if you give an inch they'll take a mile. An inch of what, you ask? Uhh ... yarn, probably.

You MUST establish dominance, put clear boundaries in place, and be consistent! Therefore, you'll be the one who decides:

- what time dinner will be served
- where you'll sleep and when
- who can approach you and under what circumstances
- how long your chosen lap shall remain stationary
- when (if ever) Russell Crowe should be forgiven for 'singing' in *Les Misérables*.

If anyone tries to coerce you into doing things their way,* simply ignore them and stand (or sit) strong. You may have moments of doubt, or at times feel like you're being harsh, but do not waver. Good person-parenting means brave leadership and a firm paw. Your human needs to feel safe under your charge.

if your human is not concerned ...

Whatever it is, it's probably fine. See something weird? Look at your human. Do they look bothered? Are their eyes open? Are they even conscious? If not, you probably don't need to take any action. Don't make a big deal out of it.

If something strange happens and you start looking all stressed and concerned, your human will pick up on this and begin to freak out, too. A freaked-out human is insufferable at the best of times, so it's important to remain calm. Only alert your human in case of a real emergency, and use your discretion to decide what qualifies as one. Here are a few examples:

Water slowly covering the entire floor? Meh, sleep somewhere high.

Intruder taking a bunch of stuff? Just don't let them touch your fur.

Kitchen going up in flames? Mmm, toasty and warm.

A bug appears? **ALERT THE HUMAN!**

*unless 'their way' directly benefits you, e.g. earlier dinner times, extra neck scritches

part two
welcome home

adopting means adapting

Sure, you're the one generously adopting a human, but it's not as simple as just slotting them in around your current life and expecting things to stay the same. Your human will need you to **adapt** to them – this means moving into their already established home, because that's where they keep all their crap. Unfortunately, it's rarely the other way around – humans really do come with a lot of belongings, way too many to fit into a shelter cage, pen or upturned garbage bin.

When you finally get your bearings in your new home, take your time getting to know the place and familiarising yourself with your new surroundings. It's good to know what you're sitting on, and where your boundaries lie. Houses come in all shapes and sizes, but most of them have at least a kitchen, a bathroom and a bedroom. You'll get to know each room and the role it plays in your human's behaviour over time as you settle in.

Check out these typical human homes. Which one do you see yourself living in?

APARTMENT

STANDARD HOUSE

FANCY HOUSE

Don't be sad to leave the place you were born ...

... it likely blows chunks compared to the new home that awaits you!

the first five days

day one

When moving into your new human's home, it's important to start small. Having access to the entire house on day one is a terrible idea – way too overwhelming! Feline best practice is to confine yourself to a small, closed room, away from chaos. A laundry, spare room, closed storage space under the stairs, or a rarely used bathroom will be the perfect spot for you to set up camp.

It's important your new human leaves you alone for a while, no matter how adorable you are, or how tempted they may be to scoop you up and present you to the sky like HRH Simba. Your heart rate needs to slow down and you MUST relax – it's been quite a day, after all. Don't worry, your human will be fine on their own until you get your bearings.

Don't be alarmed if your appetite disappears. As the gravity of this huge life-altering decision you've made begins to sink in, it's normal to feel too terrified to eat or drink. In this new environment, you'll need to feel safe and get yourself together before you can let your guard down and start stuffing your face. Same goes for pooping (though you might wanna do a little panic wee if the mood strikes).

Rest assured, your appetite and bladder control will soon return, and you'll move onto the next phase: tepid curiosity.

> REMEMBER: You can't tip water from an empty glass!
>
> To care for a human, you first need to care for yourself. You'll be of no use to anyone if you can't get your literal poop together.
>
> Don't make any sudden moves: take your time to settle in properly and feel secure before you jump headfirst into someone's lap.

day two

Your first night was probably sleepless and spooky as hell. This is normal. You almost forgot your human existed, didn't you? Or maybe you hoped it was all a dream. Make no mistake: this is your life now.

Hopefully your human provided adequate accommodations, and you're at least curious about what lies beyond the dark corner or tight spot you've squeezed yourself into. You may or may not feel like eating today. Don't pressure yourself.

Make sure your human knows you're there. With any luck, their instincts will kick in and they'll come looking for you. They'll probably give you a soft pat or a quiet cuddle, and maybe even try to play with you. These are all good, very normal human things to do. You're doing great.

Don't go nuts with reciprocation, though. You just met. Play it cool.

day three

By now you should have calmed down a bit and started eating and drinking. If not, something is wrong. Staying hydrated and keeping your strength up is key to survival, so don't be a silly goose. Genuinely not hungry? Look around you. What's happening? What's the threat?

Small child not leaving you alone? Meow in its face.

Large dog watching your every move? Sharpen your claws and start swiping.

Another cat pulling faces at you? Pull a more impressive face right back.

No food in your bowl? Time to begin putting your human to work.

You HAVE to start establishing your presence in this house NOW. Time is of the essence. You've been here three days, it's enough already. Don't forget you own this joint, and your new human needs you. Stop slacking off and get down to business. You've got this.

day four

Once you have accepted that this is your life now and you are no longer terrified by every noise and smell, it's time to suss out your surroundings. The best way to familiarise yourself with your new home is by doing a thorough perimeter check.

Maybe you are not at the point where you've seen every room of the house yet, and that's ok. But by now you should be venturing in and out of a few of the main areas where your human spends most of their time. They are going to need your supervision, so you can't afford to be irresponsible or slack off (just yet).

To perform a perimeter check, proceed slowly and simply sniff your way through it. It's mostly straightforward, though sometimes there are corners. Walk the whole interior length of the dwelling, sticking close to the outer walls. Check all doors and windows, and make sure the place is secure. If it's not secure, you have a few options:

1. LEG IT

Only do this if you really feel like you can't handle the responsibility and you've made a huge mistake. DO NOT JUST RUN OFF FOR THE FUN OF IT IF YOU PLAN TO RETURN. Your human may think you've abandoned them and search for another cat to take care of them.

It's also worth noting that you probably aren't familiar with the area, so taking off without a proper plan in mind isn't the smartest idea.

2. BRING IT TO ATTENTION

Finding an unsecured area can be a golden opportunity to showcase your skills early on, and reassure your human that they're in good paws.

Your human will probably be staring at you nonstop because they cannot believe with their own eyes how exceptionally beautiful you are. This means you can basically just stop in front of the security breach and stare at it without moving.

Your human's natural curiosity and desperate need to know everything will soon take over, and they'll poke their bald, dry nose in to sort it out.

If for some reason your human is not studying your every move, you can try meowing loudly to get their attention, or making pained, disturbing crying noises. If they still fail to acknowledge the security breach, remember this rule: IF THE HUMAN IS NOT CONCERNED, DON'T MAKE A BIG DEAL OUT OF IT (see 'basic rules of paw', page 21).

If your human is awake, lucid and not batting an eye at the thing you've clocked, maybe it's not a security breach at all. This means it's safe to move about the area as you please. If it's an open door or window, your human sees no problem with you going outside. If it's a fire or a pool of water or something and your human isn't bothered, it may just be a feature of the house – one which can be used to your advantage (see 'optional [and not-so-optional] extras', page 37).

3. IGNORE IT AND HOPE IT RESOLVES ITSELF

This is the preferred option, and great practice for adulthood. As you get older, you will realise that the vast majority of human-centric happenings are best left ignored. This doesn't mean you have to stop being curious – it just means you don't have to give a crap.

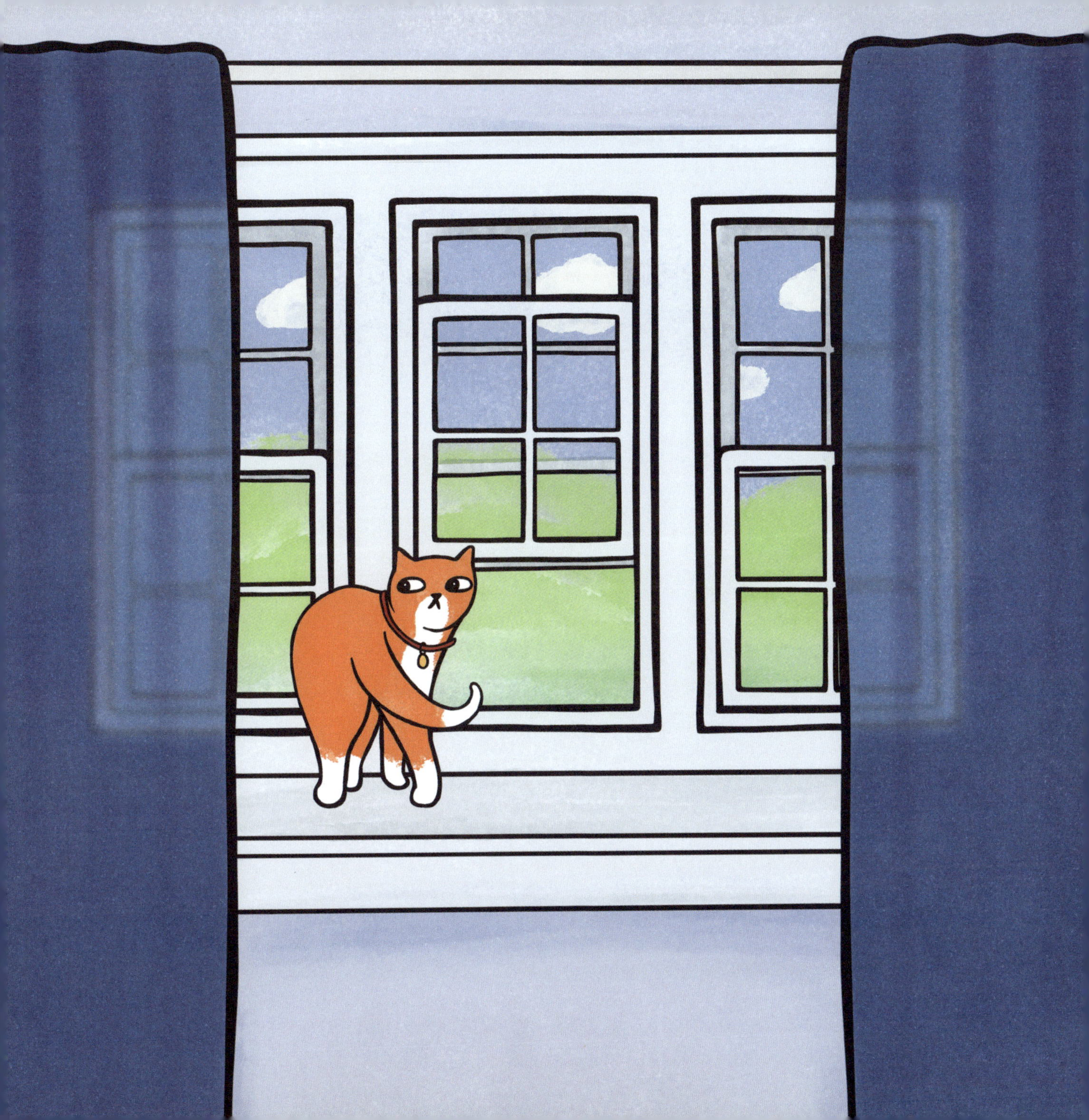

day five

Woo hoo! This marks your first official day in your new role as a person-parent! Congrats! You did it!*

By now you're definitely not shy about making your presence known, and if you are, why? You're here! You've come so far! You are set in stone as a member of this family now, no matter how big or small that family may be. In some cases, you might even be the reason it BECAME a family! Your power is immense – it's undeniable – and there's no going back now.

Of course, every human is unique and your first five days might look a little different from the ones described here. Don't worry if you're still not ready to be a person-parent after your first week, or even your first month. Humans are weird, and you're right to be cautious.

If there are any rooms you haven't seen yet, find a way to gain access. If there's anyone you haven't met yet, stare at them from a distance and psych them out. If there's any object that interests you, don't be shy about tapping it with your paw.

Now you've adopted a human, like it or not, things just can't be all about you – for a few minutes, at least. So settle that booty in, it's time to begin!

> Remember the 3-3-3 rule when adopting ...
> On average, it takes a human
> 3 DAYS to settle into being adopted,
> 3 WEEKS to learn your routine, and
> 3 MONTHS to make you sole heir of their fortune.

*'it' = You reached the starting line. Yes, that's correct. Person-parenting is a lifetime gig. Did you not realise that? Oops.

what to expect from your new abode

A concerning number of humans think a big, fancy house is better than a more modest abode. However, when all is said and done, the floor area of your home is actually much less significant than the usable vertical space it provides. What does this mean? Running around space is fine, but jumping/climbing zones are way more desirable (see helpful diagram, below). Sure, zoomies are fun across a large expanse, but have you ever zoomed upwards? Do yourself a favour and try it. Any shelf, table or semi-flat surface is your playground and you are a natural master of parkour.

Over the next few pages you'll be taken on a tour of typical rooms that are found in most human homes. If any of these are missing from yours, it's not a big deal. You may notice that where you live, some of these rooms have been combined into one, and that's ok too. Sometimes a kitchen and living room are one space. Sometimes a bathroom is attached to a bedroom. Great! These combinations make perfect sense. But if the toilet is in the kitchen, or your human's bed is in the bathtub, you might want to consider backing out of the adoption and look at getting a refund.

space to run all day like a bored dog

space to jump & climb like a majestic cat

If you have the luxury of choosing a home, ask yourself: 'How high could I possibly climb here? Is there a glass ceiling?' Ooft, imagine the birds!

living room

The name 'living room' implies the existence of an alternate 'dying room'.
If the smells are any indication, that's probably the bathroom.

bedroom

Humans, deciding to restrict themselves to only one bed, have labelled this the 'bedroom'. Super original. This room is also where humans keep their clothes, as well as a few other questionable objects.

bathroom

The 'bathroom' is a strange and dangerous place where humans disrobe and cats get wet. Avoid this room. Although ... the toilet is an interesting bowl to drink water from, and the bathtub can be an absolute pee palace if you're feeling stressed. 10/10 cats highly recommend and would pee here again.

kitchen

Arguably the most fascinating room in the house, the kitchen is a magical place where food supply is endless and counter space is coveted. There are levels to jump, deep cupboards for doing secret deeds, and hidden danger lurking in the most unexpected of stainless-steel appliances.

Do yourself a favour and memorise the layout of your kitchen carefully, especially your own food cupboard. You will need to guide your human there on a daily basis to remind them where it is. They forget, you see.

The kitchen has other stuff in it, too. It's where humans prepare their own food, which they fuss over quite a lot. The oven, which looks like a nice cosy place to sit, is actually a blistering inferno. Stay away from it. It has actual fire coming out the top, so stay away from that too. The sink is moody and spits water on occasion, but if you're brave enough to go in when it's dormant, you can sometimes find little food scraps in there.

But perhaps the most important thing about this room is something so magical it can't be restricted to just one page ...

> If you don't usher your human to the food cupboard each and every dinner time (plus offer additional refresher reminders throughout the day), there's a high chance you'll starve to death. Don't risk it, bro.

BEHOLD!
the mystical food portal

the belly of the beast

The mystical food portal is a bizarre, space-age chamber of sorts, and is referred to by humans as **F.R.I.D.G.E.** We believe the name stands for **Food Readily Instant and Double Good Eating.** Why space-age? It's cold and has an airlock. Duh.

F.R.I.D.G.E. is pretty exclusive and very hard to get into. The door only opens for seconds at a time at irregular intervals throughout the day, so there is really no preparing yourself for the chance to get a closer inspection.

If you're lucky enough to catch a glimpse inside, F.R.I.D.G.E. will waste no time shining its light on you, pulling you into a state of involuntary hypnosis. As your eyes adjust, it will reveal to you an array of exotic bottles, glimmering jars and fetid containers, leaving your mouth agape and adrool at the sheer sensory overload of it all ... until suddenly the door slams shut again and breaks the creepy spell, leaving you wondering how many lives you have left.

Those who have ventured inside (and survived to talk about it) have recounted chilling tales of rogue zucchinis, gigantic blocks of cheese, and weird sticky substances dripping from the sky. It remains, to this day, one of the greatest mysteries of our time.

common (and not-so-common) features

outdoor area

The vast majority of humans seem bothered when a cat goes outside. These humans will actively try to stop you from leaving the house and there are several reasons that may justify this creepy, possessive behaviour:

1. They are extremely jealous. They don't want you meeting other humans you might like more than them.
2. The idea of you, their commandant, roaming unprotected in the outside world frightens them. What if something happened to you and they had to fend for themselves?
3. They live to serve you, so they'd rather run your outdoor errands themselves than have you lift a paw.
4. Something about wildlife. Maybe they think lizards are dangerous or something. Cute.

It might seem weird or unnatural at first to live your nine lives exclusively indoors, but admittedly it's for the best. Being outside can increase your risk of sunburn (yes, even under all that luscious fur), and if you're the type to defend your human's honour, you could be injured by fighting with other cats.

If you're more of a lover than a fighter, spending a lot of time outdoors (especially at night) could increase your chances of contracting viruses or even having kittens.

> Bruh. Don't even think about going out and making kittens. You've got enough in your bowl right now. There's no sense jeopardising it.

private catio

By far the most impressive thing you can train your human to do is construct a private catio just for you. It's truly the best of both worlds: fresh air, infinite smells, live dinner theatre, al fresco pooping ... and no predators!

It's basically your own private retreat away from the responsibilities of person-parenting. A well-designed catio will have places to climb, things to scratch and discreet holes to hide in. You can even bring your favourite toy back there for some private cuddle time, away from prying human eyes.

Sure, other neighbourhood cats who aren't so lucky may visit and taunt you. Sure, they may call you a wuss who can't handle the real world. Sure, they might poop right upwind of the spot where your food bowl is. But they're probably just trying to drown out their pesky internal monologue constantly reminding them that the reason they don't have a catio is because they've failed as a person-parent, and more so, as a cat.

optional (and not-so-optional) extras

CARDBOARD BOXES
temporary play centres providing hours of fun!

FIREPLACE
literally a hole in the wall full of fire, so your tail might catch alight if you get too close (kinda worth it)

KENNEL
poorly decorated, uninsulated stink hole

TREE HOUSE
because nothing is just for you anymore, not even trees

POOL
nope

SAND PIT
an other-worldly pooping experience

making your house a home

redecorating

This is your new living area, so it needs to be a comfortable and relaxing place. Hopefully your human will have anticipated being adopted, and as part of their many preparations to maximise their chances of acceptance, they'll have added a few new pieces to their home prior to your arrival.

Your human should have at least installed a couple of scratching posts, a window hammock, climbing ropes or panels, multi-levelled jump steps, a deluxe windowsill sleeper, a sky bed and maybe a ceiling superhighway – perhaps just a basic model with a suspension bridge and rest port to start with, until you get settled in. If not, you might have adopted a peasant. Oh well, good karma for you!

Whether they went the extra mile or not with stuff for you, you will probably notice that your human's own design taste is lacking. It's not their fault. They have limited resources and they're doing their best – so try to remember that before you totally poo-poo their choices. Or on them. Your human is counting on you to guide them, so if you can't be nice, at least be subtle.

Anything can be a scratching post if you're adventurous enough ...

A great place to start redecorating is with furnishings. The couch is basically begging for rejuvenation, so start shredding the living heck out of it as a matter of high importance. Coat the top back section with your fur until it resembles a sort of throw rug. See? Immediate improvement.

Clawing the crap out of things is a natural stress reliever, so make this a priority. If no scratching posts have been provided for you, simply create your own. Sure, couches are the logical first choice, but you'll have plenty of other options if you're creative and brave enough to try.

The next thing you'll want to do is teach your human good tidying habits. Make them rearrange a few things. Don't like seeing charger cables lying around? Chew them. Annoyed by half-empty glasses left on tables? Knock them down. Sick of your human leaving their bum-wipe rolls on display? Shred them.

As for any pictures on the wall, give it time. Soon most, if not all, of these will be replaced with pictures of you, dramatically improving the aesthetic just by existing in the space.

traversing tricky obstacles

is your human shutting you out?

At some point your human may rebel and want their own space. This is unacceptable and you should never stand OR sit for it. If you notice your human start closing the internal doors of your house with you on the other side, it means they are actively hiding something from you.

As a person-parent, you have a duty of care towards your human. You should know what they are doing every single second they spend under your roof. Who knows what they'll get up to if you're not watching them, or at least spying on them from the comfort of a half-nap?

However, all is not lost, because doors can be defeated. In most cases, it's not the actual door you have to contend with: it's the knob controlling it. Beating the knob = maximum satisfaction.

SWINGING DOOR
difficulty: medium/hard depending on type of closure mechanism (see below)

Jump up and use your body weight to apply pressure to the handle. Tilty handles are easiest because you only have to tilt them downwards. Round knobs require more dexterity but are not impossible to conquer.

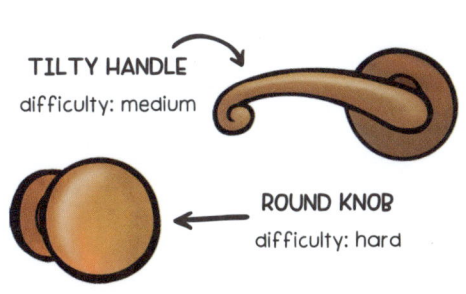

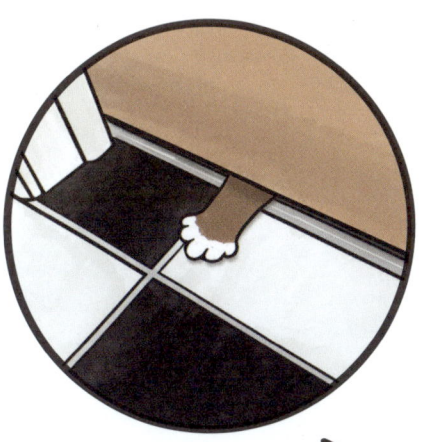

TILTY HANDLE
difficulty: medium

ROUND KNOB
difficulty: hard

GAP PAW
difficulty: easy

This move is a typical command for your human to open the door on your behalf (or else).

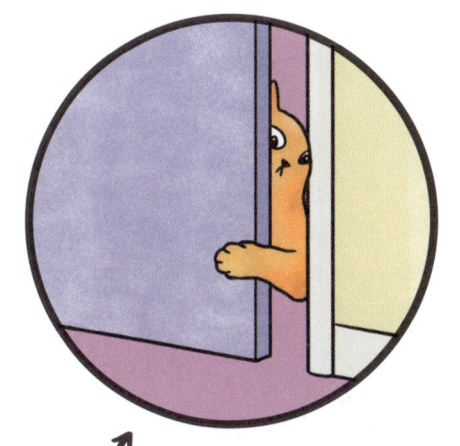

SLIDING DOOR
difficulty: easy, total piece of crab cake

Simply dig a few claws into the crack, then slide it open.

household objects of mystery & intrigue

Some (or all) of these random objects will make an appearance in your home at any given time, so be prepared. Cats have worked tirelessly for eons to understand them, but they remain a mystery to this day. Weird.

Where do they come from? Humans have been witnessed dragging them in from their travels, but while some of these items are fun to chew, they are typically not edible and serve no apparent purpose other than to taunt and mock you.

Are they gifts of some sort? Or something more sinister? Impossible to say. Some of them will bite you, whereas others will lay dormant and even play dead. Some will attach themselves to your fur, chase you around the house and terrorise you for no reason, while others will roll away and actively avoid you. Absolutely bizarre behaviour.

As you will see from the evidence collected (below), and the conspiracy board (opposite), there may be a cryptic connection between these objects. Is this some sort of warped puzzle we must solve? Will we ever find out the truth?

What is clear, though, is that most of them don't stick around long. One by one, these things will eventually gravitate towards their communal safe house in the kitchen, under the mystical food portal (page 34). Few have ever returned to see the light of day.

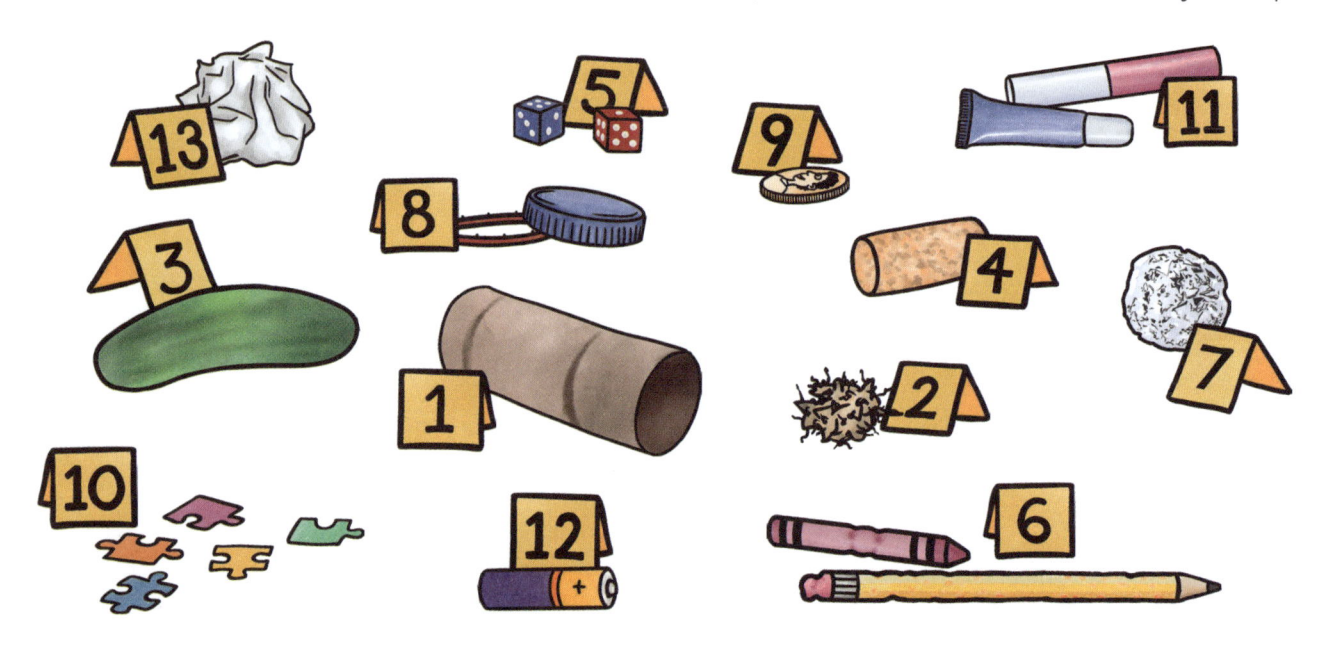

1. Found in bathroom. Passive. Gets soggy when chewed. 2. Very active. Separates and spawns when touched, dusty texture. 3. Slimy, cold to the touch. 4. Seen flying into the air then rolling around on the ground. Smells drunk. 5. Crunchy. 6. Chewy, but you can't eat a lot of it, you know? 7. Endless combat, will sometimes blind you. 8. Deranged duo working as a team, will sometimes divide and conquer. Skinny one attaches to paw?? Hard to shake off. Wide one sometimes tastes like milk. 9. No. 10. Appears to be some sort of gang. 11. Witnessed escaping from handbag. Omits a strange liquid when chewed. 12. Rolly. Low chewability. Possibly related to board sample B. 13. May contain sensitive information. Becomes soggy and disintegrates when chewed (possible self-destruct function).

unprovoked attacks
traces of human hair detected
human carries this. WHY??
some sort of aural obsession??
connection to human ear?
discovered in unattended bag
countless victims found **soiled and maimed** in nearby garbage bin
ENTANGLEMENT
BLATANT ASSAULT OF INNOCENT CATS!!
known triggers:
chewing
licking
SAMPLE B
why is it spicy?
highly chewable
I've stumbled on a conspiracy here. Look at all this stuff! It's all connected! This is not some innocent random occurrence, bro ... These things are in drawers! In bags! In stupid little bowls that don't even have food in them!!
Something fishy is going on here, and it sure as heck isn't ... uhh ... fish.

deadly hazards
and other things to watch out for

STICKY TAPE
sly, transparent psychopath that will attach itself to a healthy host, must be forceably and painfully removed and will take a piece of you with it

SPRAY BOTTLE
stealthy mother-fluffer not to be reckoned with, shoots stream of poison from afar with unsettling precision

VACUUM
loud, obnoxious lunatic who is hell-bent on sucking your soul and/or tail whilst groaning inappropriately and thrusting back and forth

BROOM
designed to move dirt around and mock you – will pretend to be dead when stationary before coating you with filth

MOP
dirt-licking weirdo, always oddly moist – keep your distance

LINT ROLLER
total creeper – sticky, rolls around hoarding fur, then wears it like some kind of serial killer

person-parent essentials

You already know that to care for a human, you must first take care of yourself. You're not going to be of use to anyone if you're a grotty, uncomfortable mess all the time.

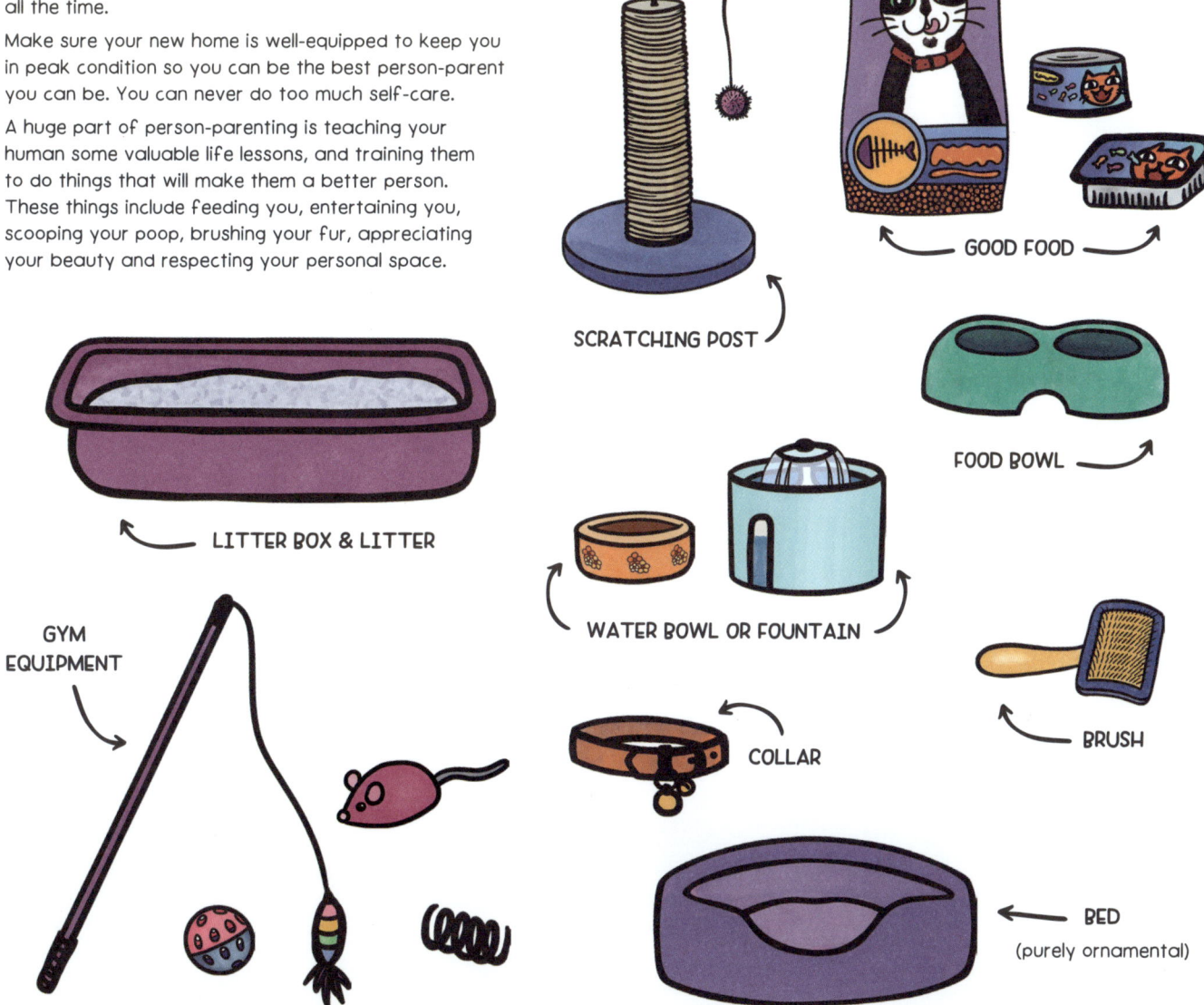

Make sure your new home is well-equipped to keep you in peak condition so you can be the best person-parent you can be. You can never do too much self-care.

A huge part of person-parenting is teaching your human some valuable life lessons, and training them to do things that will make them a better person. These things include feeding you, entertaining you, scooping your poop, brushing your fur, appreciating your beauty and respecting your personal space.

SCRATCHING POST

GOOD FOOD

FOOD BOWL

LITTER BOX & LITTER

WATER BOWL OR FOUNTAIN

BRUSH

GYM EQUIPMENT

COLLAR

BED
(purely ornamental)

part three

understanding your human

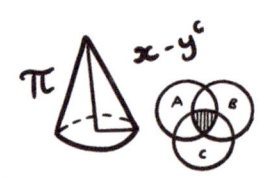

human essentials

Now that you've settled in and made yourself comfortable, it's time to start doing some actual person-parenting. No, this doesn't just mean acknowledging your human briefly in passing between meals (yet) – there's more work to be done before you can fully relax and let yourself go. It's time to start taking responsibility for your adoptee and the huge, life-altering decision you've made – no take-backsies.

According to some cat called Mewslow,* humans come with a 'Hierarchy of Needs' (right). Other names that were spit-balled for this model but didn't make the cut included 'Structure for Cats Adopting Miscreants' (SCAM) and 'Meowing Loudly Matters' (MLM).

Ok, yes, sure, it does look like a bit of a pyramid scheme, and it might be pyramid-shaped. Does this mean you're about to get sucked into loving a human forever? Look, it's a possibility. But it's too late to back out now (no take-backsies, remember?), so just settle in, accept your fate, and let the ambiguous promised benefits pay off somewhere down the line. Potentially.

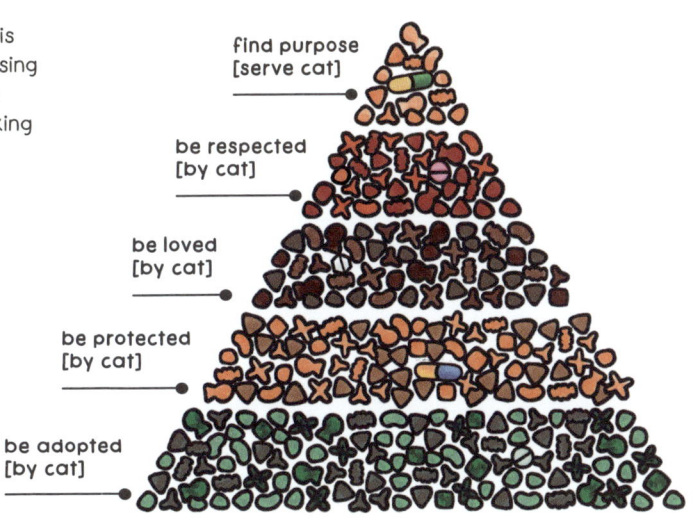

- find purpose [serve cat]
- be respected [by cat]
- be loved [by cat]
- be protected [by cat]
- be adopted [by cat]

According to this Mewslow and his sophisticated triangle, humans have five basic requirements in order to survive. He says the lower-level needs have to be met before the higher ones can be fulfilled, which means that by adopting a human, you're already on the right track! Yay! Go you!

But what does the rest of this obtusely angled obelisk mean? How will you level up? Is there some sort of boss you have to uppercut at the end of each stage to get to the next one? What's the reward? Is it even achievable to grow a decent human being who can function (or at least appear to function) properly in this world?

Clearly a more detailed explanation is needed, preferably in the form of a PowerPoint presentation ...

Perhaps you'd feel more at ease if this ominous-looking prism was subtly redesigned to resemble something less confronting and not laced with medication ... How about, say, a sort of textured, scratchable Multi-Level Mat?

I got you, fam. Next page. Go.

*or someone who looks a bit like him. Could've been his cousin.

45

Mewslow's hierarchy of human needs

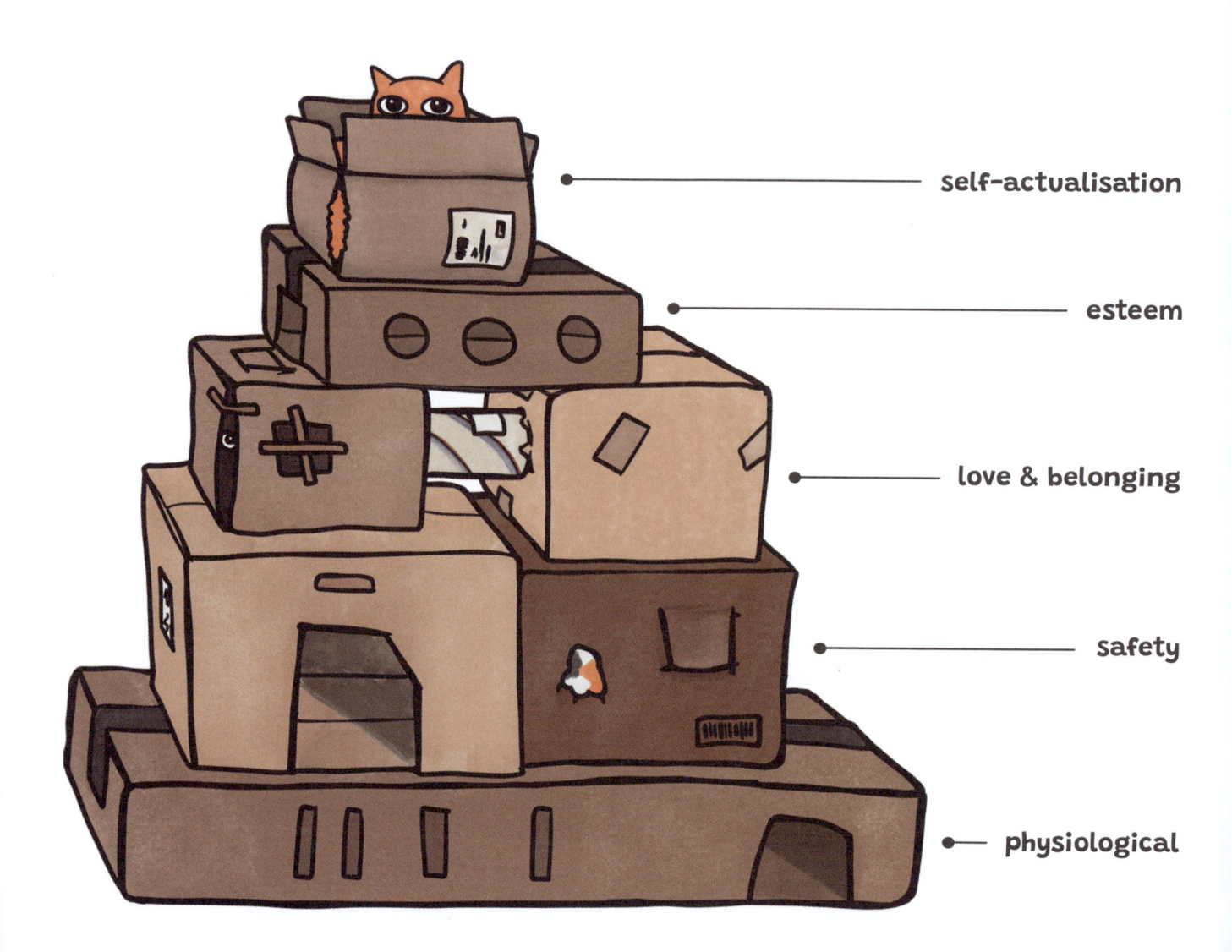

- self-actualisation
- esteem
- love & belonging
- safety
- physiological

1. PHYSIOLOGICAL – be adopted by a cat

Humans are 100% dependent on cats. At a fundamental biological level, humans need cats to survive in the same way they need water and food.

Being adopted by a cat is a human's ticket to survival, and the absolute baseline for living. Think about the cat-less humans you've seen – they wander aimlessly, without purpose. They try to fool others by bragging about all their freedom and how much they travel and why being adopted simply wouldn't be feasible right now, but they're not even having a good time. Nobody is buying it.

2. SAFETY – be protected by a cat

Humans are suboptimal hunters because they live in fear. They rely on their feline protectors to keep them safe from the threats of the outside world. You can do this by catching intruder bugs, conducting regular perimeter checks of your home, and glaring at passers-by from the window.

3. LOVE & BELONGING – be loved by a cat

The love of a cat gives humans a feeling they can't replicate, no matter how hard they try. Once they've experienced the human-cat bond, they'll likely never feel complete again without it. To show love, throw them a leg rub, a snuggle, some lap biscuits, or even just an upthrust-tail greeting and friendly chirrup once in a while.

4. ESTEEM – be respected by a cat

This one is probably the toughest level to complete, which is probably why it's second from the top. But remember – your human only has to THINK you respect them. Next time they bust your ass for being on the kitchen counter, humour them and jump down (you can jump back up when they leave).

5. SELF-ACTUALISATION – find purpose (serve a cat)

Serving a cat gives your human a sense of significance that unlocks all kinds of capabilities. Suddenly they realise why they have a lap! Thumbs are perfect for opening food tins! Who knew?! It's almost as if your human was completely useless until a cat came into their life.

your roles & responsibilities

By now you may be asking yourself, 'What is my role in my human's life? Why did I adopt them in the first place? What part do I play in their day-to-day existence? What does my human expect and need from me? What the hell have I done? Was this a huge mistake? How am I going to get out of this?' and so on, and so forth.

Yes, being a person-parent comes with a lot of questions, most of which do not have answers. Is this helpful? No. But will this journey you've embarked on be a rewarding and satisfying experience that will change you for the better and make you a more caring feline being in the long run? Also no. But at the very least there's shelter, warmth and free food, which is a good enough place to start.

Listen, if you're going into adoption thinking you can keep living the way you like and your human will just 'slot in around you', think again. They won't slot in; they will tiptoe so they don't wake you. Parenting is tiring, and you need your rest.

Responsible person-parenting, if done right, can actually be a fairly cushy job. While it's true that a lot of different duties are involved, most of them are easy to learn.

The job description below outlines just some of the roles you'll be required to play. At first glance it may seem like a lot, but caring for a human is one of those rare jobs you can half-ass and still look competent. Humans are easily fooled, you see.

Besides, being at home all day with a human is a way better gig than Stinky Stray or Big-Fat-Kitten-Factory. You'll be fine.

job description

HEAT PACK — keep human warm in winter, be on call year-round for cramps

SURFACE AUDITOR — evict undesirable items from shelving or tabletops

CUS-TOE-DIAN — keep rogue digits in check

WORK OF ART — soothe human's eyes with regular appearances

PERSONAL MOTIVATOR — wake human up early, make them do things

BACKUP HUNTER — catch food for human when they appear incompetent

MEAL INSPECTOR — quality-check human food, rectify mistakes

SECURITY GUARD — perform perimeter checks, spy on people

TERRITORY CONSULTANT — perform stocktake, mark scent on all belongings

mental health support

The easiest task for a cat to perform, which you might already be doing without realising, is to provide mental health support.

You see, the human brain is way too large and not very energy efficient (see page 71). Some brains keep all that extra space empty, but other brains will fill it with all manner of junk like anxiety, trauma, comedy and other unpleasantries. There are human brains that even attack themselves, which is clearly a problematic design flaw.

Sure, at times you may be the one to cause some of the issues your adopted human is struggling with, like hiding for long periods of time, not coming back at night, or ripping off your collar and/or tracking device and leaving it in a dog kennel next to a chunk of your fur and a splatter of blood. But, for the most part, even just your presence can be very therapeutic, not to mention aesthetically pleasing.

motivate and activate

Does your human have, say, a book to write but is hiding under the covers, crying about it instead? Does your human need to feed themselves – and you – but can't get out of bed?

Demand food. Even if you're not hungry. Give them a reason to get up.

Do they need to take their meds? Find that pill bottle and play soccer with it on a tile floor until the noise alone causes a sensory overload and attracts your human's attention.

Is your human sad? Acknowledge them briefly and look concerned. When your human asks, 'How did you know I needed a cuddle?' play it cool and lead them to the food cupboard.

cuddles, consent & you

meow means meow!

One thing a lot of humans overlook when going in for a smooch is the importance of consent. Sure, when you're in the mood, a well-placed pat can be the greatest thing in the world! However, if you don't want to be touched and a human is insisting, things can get real ugly, real fast.

If your human really loves you, they will accept and respect your cuddle style. Don't let yourself be pressured or guilted into smooches. Remember: you are the boss of your own body – no exceptions.*

Fortunately, the same cannot be said the other way around. Humans will take your cuddles, even if they don't want them, because they know attention from a cat is the highest honour. Once they get it, they will do almost anything to keep it.

Remember: AFFECTION = POWER!

If it's a cold morning and you don't want your human to leave the house, simply settle on their lap. They will be unable to move until you decide it's time.

Feel free to borrow my mantra anytime you need it ...

Don't pet me if you just met me

*A thermometer-wielding vet may deem themselves the exception to this rule. See page 104 for how to deal with this type of human.

typical affection styles

SHOULDER SMOOCH
comfy in small doses, option to dig claws in if you get scared

CLUTCH 'N' SQUEEZE
popular with young humans, also goes by the name 'Internal Organ Bachata'

CLASSIC HEAD BUMP
scent-marking made easy

STANDING BUM-HOLD
good support, human's arm acts as a handy chin/paw rest

SIMBA
not as prestigious as it looks

REVERSE SIMBA
like the regular simba but with a less flattering view

so you're just not that into them (common)

Let's face it. Some humans just plain suck. You're not going to get along with everyone – that's just a fact. So how do you tell a human you're not into them?

It can be quite tricky, mostly because so many humans have massive egos and a creepy need to be liked. They seem to care a lot what others think about them, and despite their outward self-confidence, most of them are extremely insecure.

Humans are not enlightened enough to understand that this is a terrible waste of their time. Can you imagine having only one life instead of nine? Wild. And worse – spending that singular life worrying about nonsense like what others think about them? ABSOLUTE MADNESS! That's why they need us in the first place.

But you can't be everything to everyone, so it's imperative you are clear when letting them know it's not going to work out.*

sending a clear message of disdain
Subtle yet effective ways to deter a human.

- violently swish tail
- expose claws
- hiss and/or growl
- leave the room

how to make a human bugger off already
If they're not getting the hint, it may be time to ramp things up!

- pee on them
- fart on them
- bite them (deep chomp)
- scratch them

*Of course if you prefer, you can simply forget all this and lead them on, only to drop them at a later date. Playing mind games with humans is loads of fun, and not difficult at all.

learning to live with disappointment

If your human really won't budge and you can't be bothered running away and finding a new one, you run the risk of living out the rest of your nine lives with resentment. This is not a huge adjustment, but it can be tiring.

Instead, why not consider upcycling your human? It may be worth your while to find other uses for them you hadn't previously thought of.

alternative uses for your human

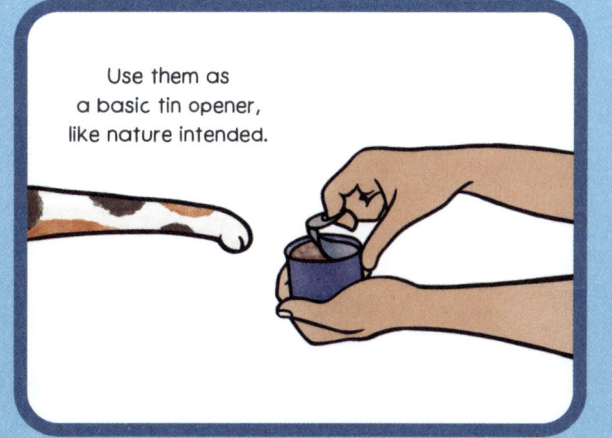

Use them as a climbing apparatus or vaulting platform.

Rub up against their legs to dislodge bugs and dirt stuck in your fur.

Use them as a source of warmth in winter (sleep on their face).

Use them as a basic tin opener, like nature intended.

so they're just not that into you (rare)

forcing a human to love you

It seems unfathomable, but picture this (highly unlikely) scenario: A live-in associate of a human you've chosen says they 'don't want a(nother) damn cat!!' Shocking, right? But there's a slim chance it could happen to you, so be prepared.

There's nothing more satisfying than converting a **NOPE** (Not Open to Puss Entertaining) into a **YEP** (Yielding Embracer of Puss). Typically, you'll find this kind of person as an extension of the human you initially adopted. They will likely live in the same house and be totally averse to the idea of you moving in. Dads and dad-figures are historically the usual offenders here, though any human who fancies themselves as big and tough and too good for feelings could be guilty of the same.

It may sound daunting, but these particular humans are actually some of the easiest to convert. Deep down inside, they are quite cat-like themselves. They just need someone to relate to. That's where you come in.

extreme reluctance

Some humans really, truly, do not want to be adopted. This variety of human has limited self-awareness, and is therefore even more in need of adoption than most.

It's certainly not wrong to adopt a human against their will. While it can be a struggle to adopt an **ERD** (Extremely Reluctant Doofus), it's not impossible if you apply yourself.

the allergy cliché

Humans are not stupid – they can find a loophole just as well as we can. The unwilling human's favourite excuse not to be adopted is the tired old 'I'm allergic' trope. They don't realise that this is not a deterrent for us – merely an obstacle.

Allergies are so lame. Have you ever seen an 'allergic' human? It's quite a show they put on. They really get into it – sneezing, eyes watering (crying), even scratching or claiming they can't breathe. Ugh, grow up. If they're insisting on being special, they can easily dose up on meds, use air filters or try immunotherapy.

---

ways to induce acceptance

1. Spy on them (at a respectful distance). If they catch you, pretend to sniff a plant or something.

2. Go hard on interference. Are they watching TV? Stand in front of it. Making coffee? Introduce them to Señor MilkPaw.

3. Give them the signal as a test. If they don't respond appropriately, repeat (1) and (2) until they do.

Before long, the resistant human will get used to your presence, and begin to naturally associate you with their day-to-day existence. They will then subtly start seeking you out, and may even worry if they lose sight of you (though they'll probably act unbothered).

Eventually, when you feel the time is right (don't worry – you'll just know), wait for them to fall asleep in their chair,* then gently climb into their lap, and commence Power Purr™. However, if they make the first move, leave them hanging.

*This type always has 'their chair', which will eventually end up being 'your chair'.

how to identify the stages of adoption acceptance

1 NOPE	2 ARGHH	3 C'MONNNN	4 GRUMP	5 UGH FINE
'#@*! NO!! Absolutely not! Not happening, no freaking way.'	'I get no darn respect in this house. I live here too, you know!'	'Don't I at least get a say in this?? Be reasonable!'	[silent grumble-bum energy]	'Ugh, FINE. But I want nothing to do with it, ya hear me?'

REMEMBER: First comes tolerance, then comes undying love, then comes you no longer giving a toss and simply coasting off your good looks and natural charm forever.

how to identify a human who cannot possibly like you

Uh oh!
IMAGE NOT FOUND
THE ILLUSTRATION YOU ARE LOOKING FOR DOES NOT EXIST

TRY SEARCHING FOR SOMETHING LESS RIDICULOUS

communication
understanding human speech and deciphering gestures

Humans do not respect silence. Probably only around 0.2% of what humans say in their lifetime is relevant or mildly interesting. For this reason it is perfectly acceptable to ignore them, at least until you require their assistance.

what to respond to

The safest and only time it's necessary to respond to a human is at mealtimes. Even then, they don't really expect a response so much as a brief acknowledgement. Make sure you're responding at a proper mealtime, though – beware of false gestures like ye olde shake 'n' fake (page 101).

what to ignore

Studies by reputable cats show that ignoring your human is of little consequence and does not have adverse effects over time. If anything, it makes them respect your time even more. If your human calls your name out of the blue in the middle of the day, it will mean one or more of the following:

a. They want you to drop everything so they can order one of your finest, freshest, cuddle-smooch combo deals.

b. They've invited a guest without asking and would like to seek your approval of said guest.

c. They're going on a long hunting trip and need to alert you that your bowl has been filled at an irregular time so you won't miss dinner and/or wait up.

d. They're embarking on an even longer hunting trip and would like to say goodbye in case they don't make it back, or worse, they do make it back but without any food, hereby pre-empting your disappointment by trying to grasp at some fragile scraps of your love before it all goes south.

e. They're about to load you into the dreaded cramped condo and whisk you off to the vet.

All of the above can and should be ignored, except for option 'A' (if you're into that sort of thing). You may think responding will be worth it or, on some level, offer you a sort of intellectual enrichment. It won't.

QUICK RESPOND/IGNORE GO-TO GUIDE

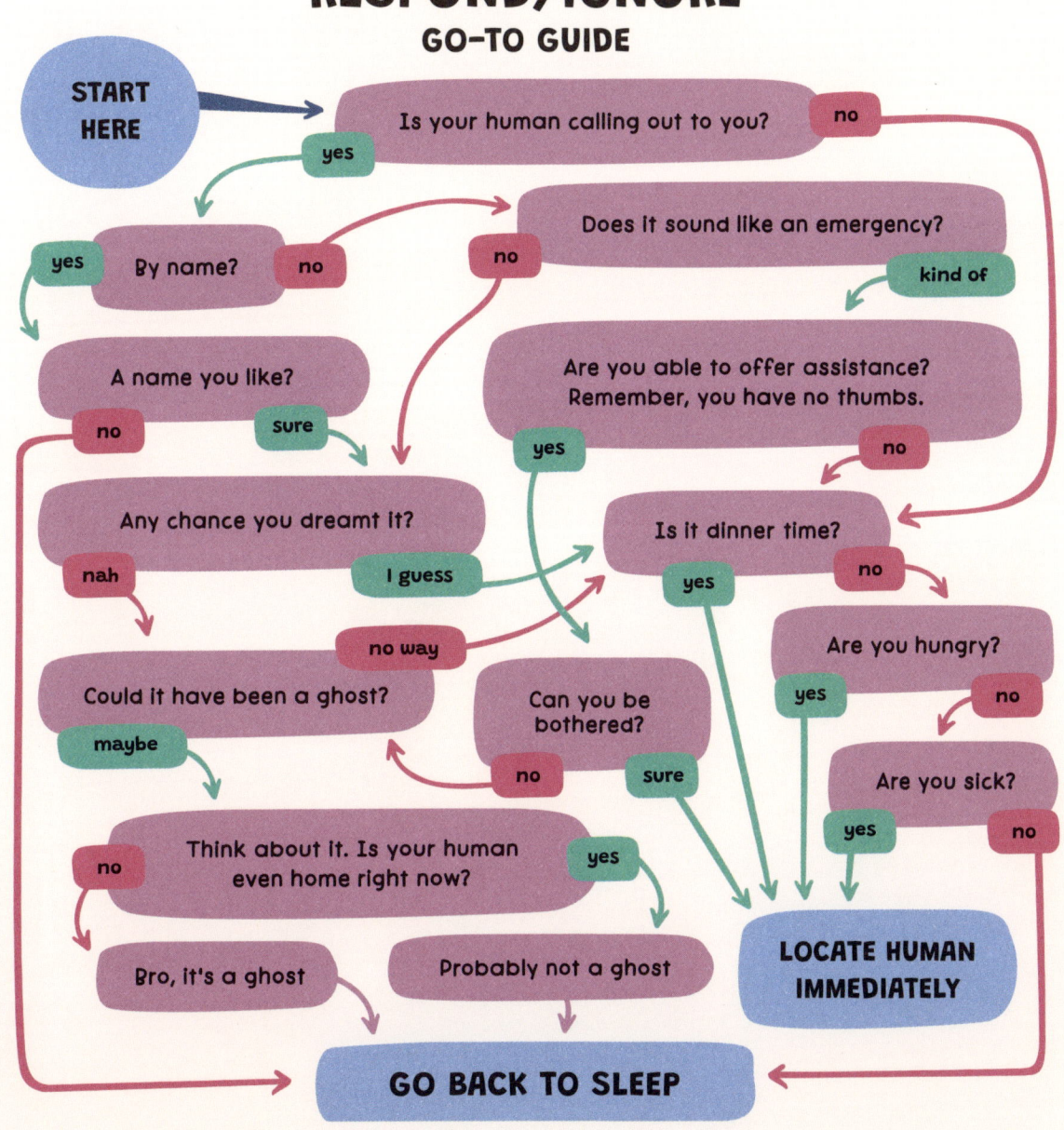

START HERE → Is your human calling out to you?
- **no** → Is it dinner time?
- **yes** → By name?
  - **yes** → A name you like?
    - **no** → GO BACK TO SLEEP
    - **sure** → Any chance you dreamt it?
  - **no** → Does it sound like an emergency?

Does it sound like an emergency?
- **no** → Any chance you dreamt it?
- **kind of** → Are you able to offer assistance? Remember, you have no thumbs.
  - **yes** → Is it dinner time?
  - **no** → Is it dinner time?

Any chance you dreamt it?
- **nah** → Could it have been a ghost?
- **I guess** → Is it dinner time?
- **no way** → Can you be bothered?

Could it have been a ghost?
- **maybe** → Think about it. Is your human even home right now?

Think about it. Is your human even home right now?
- **no** → Bro, it's a ghost
- **yes** → Probably not a ghost

Can you be bothered?
- **no** → Could it have been a ghost?
- **sure** → Is it dinner time?

Is it dinner time?
- **yes** → LOCATE HUMAN IMMEDIATELY
- **no** → Are you hungry?

Are you hungry?
- **yes** → LOCATE HUMAN IMMEDIATELY
- **no** → Are you sick?

Are you sick?
- **yes** → LOCATE HUMAN IMMEDIATELY
- **no** → GO BACK TO SLEEP

Bro, it's a ghost → GO BACK TO SLEEP
Probably not a ghost → GO BACK TO SLEEP

talking to your human about matters of great importance

Picture this: You give your human a basic command and not only do they not do it, they reply with something completely unrelated. Annoying, right? Or worse, they respond with the old condescending 'I know'. No, Susan, you don't know. You really don't. Stop embarrassing yourself.

Communication breakdowns like these are very common and can be frustrating for everyone involved. However, you don't need to resort to biting just yet, because there is a solution.

We already know that humans cannot understand basic cat – or can they? No. They can't. BUT they can understand tone.

A basic meow can be regulated to suit your needs. Humans instinctively recognise that the louder and more incessant your meow is, the more urgent your request must be. Try it! As a brilliant writer once said, 'Incessant meowing gets $*#! done.'*

Over time, your human will pick up on the tones and pitches of your different meows and learn what they mean. If not, they are either deaf or they do not respect you, which is a whole other situation ...

*She's said it more than once. She says it all the time, actually. Continuously. Incessantly, even. And she doesn't really say it, she usually yells it. Sometimes there's hissing.

what to do if your human meows back

Because you now spend sooooo much time ignoring your human, they'll begin to think you don't understand their language. They don't know you're ignoring them, they just think you can't speak human. Bless their little human-made cotton socks!

It's a fair assumption, really – you're not responding to them and all your meows sound the same to them, so what other conclusion would they come to? How are they to know you're a small genius capable of greatness beyond their wildest dreams? Sure, there are some pretty obvious signs, but still.

Unfortunately this presents a new problem where the human will attempt speaking your language instead. Yes, it sounds ridiculous, but meowing is all too common among humans who have been adopted by cats. Here's how to handle it:

1. Don't take the bait

The first time you hear your human meow back at you is a surreal experience. It's normal to be surprised, but pay them no heed – they know not what they say. Yes, some of their meows might make a little sense, but it's just dumb luck. Even if they've somehow managed to construct an entire sentence, rest assured they have no idea what they're talking about. No exceptions. Don't be fooled.

2. Play along

If you don't believe that they're oblivious to their own meows, try answering back. How did they react? Most humans will laugh or smile and get excited that you're having a conversation with them. They really are hard up for intellectual stimulation, you see.

3. Bring on the cuss

Still don't believe they can't understand you? Start cussing them out. Call them whatever you want. Did they kick you out after what you said about their mother? No! But the joke's on you – you're their mother now, you silly sausage.

> MeOw? heh

> haha mEoW!

> **DID YOU KNOW?**
> Humans think that a human meowing like a cat sounds more like a cat than a cat meowing like a cat. Pfft.

human body language
what is yours trying to tell you?

FIERCELY POINTING
'Look! I have a finger! Would you like to chomp on it?'

FLIPPING THE BIRD*
'You are cordially invited to urinate in my fresh laundry, or on my bed.'
*No real birds involved. Name is wildly misleading.

ARMS OUTSTRETCHED EXPECTANTLY
'I bet you can't fit through this gap as I close my hands at the last second.'

LOUDLY STOMPING FEET
'My ancestors were dinosaurs so this is normal, actually.'

FINGER GUNS
'I have thumbs and you don't. Ner ner.'

WHOLE HAND WAVE
'I am leaving and/or arriving. Look, I have hands instead of paws, so my hunting performance may be suboptimal.'

CLENCHED FISTS
'I'm upset that I don't have paws but if I go like this it sort of looks like I do.'

BLUSHING
'My mere existence is embarrassing. Thank you, cat, for accepting me and allowing me the opportunity for self-improvement.'

FACEPALM
'Nope, still no hair on this spot. Maybe if I keep touching it, I'll grow some and one day be almost as beautiful as my cat.'

inside the human mind

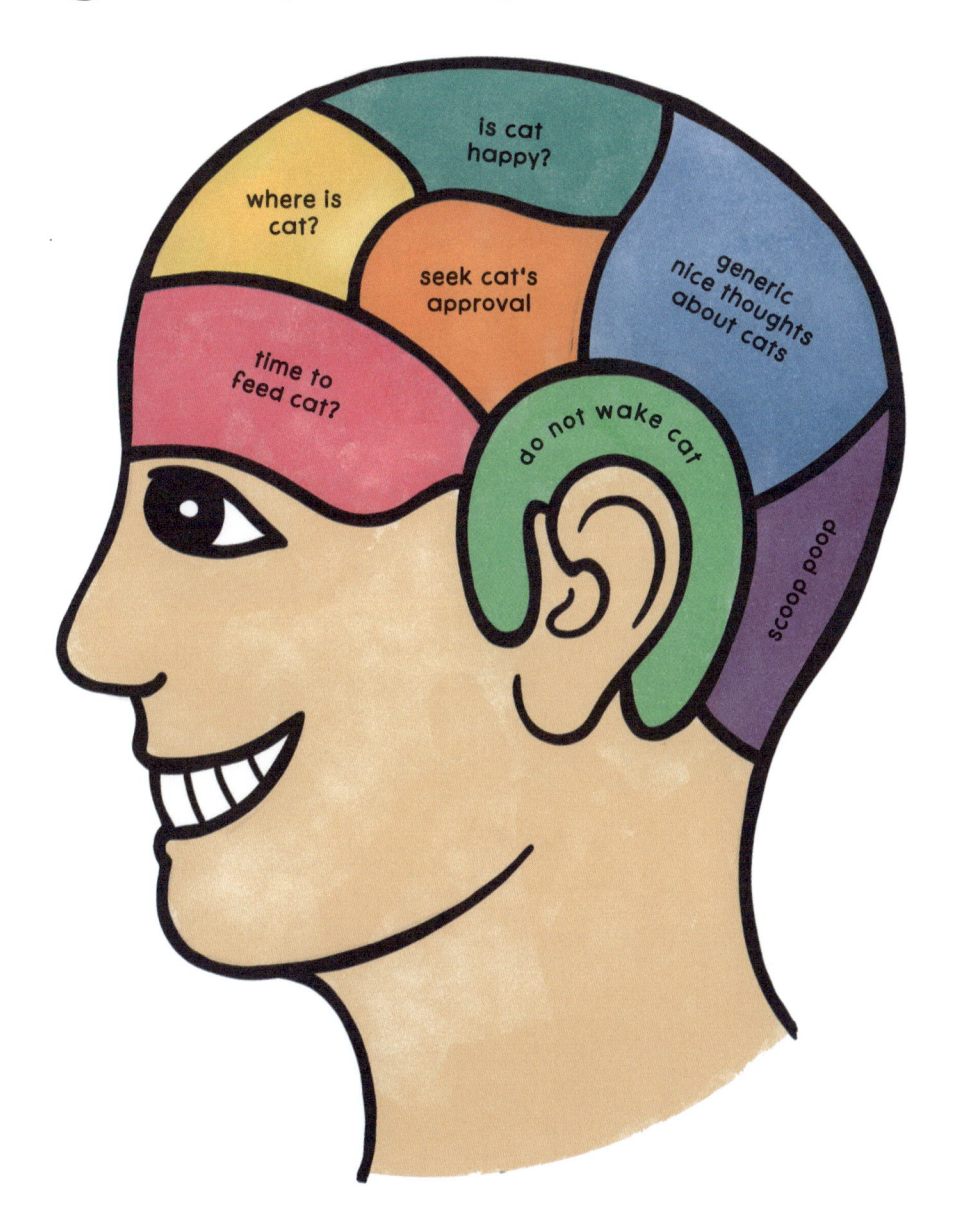

- is cat happy?
- where is cat?
- seek cat's approval
- generic nice thoughts about cats
- time to feed cat?
- do not wake cat
- scoop poop

As you can see from the image above, the phrenological faculties of the human being revolve solely around us. Therefore, one can surmise that by adopting humans and letting them serve us, we are actually fulfilling their needs on a primal level.

part four
human quirks & characteristics

the human body

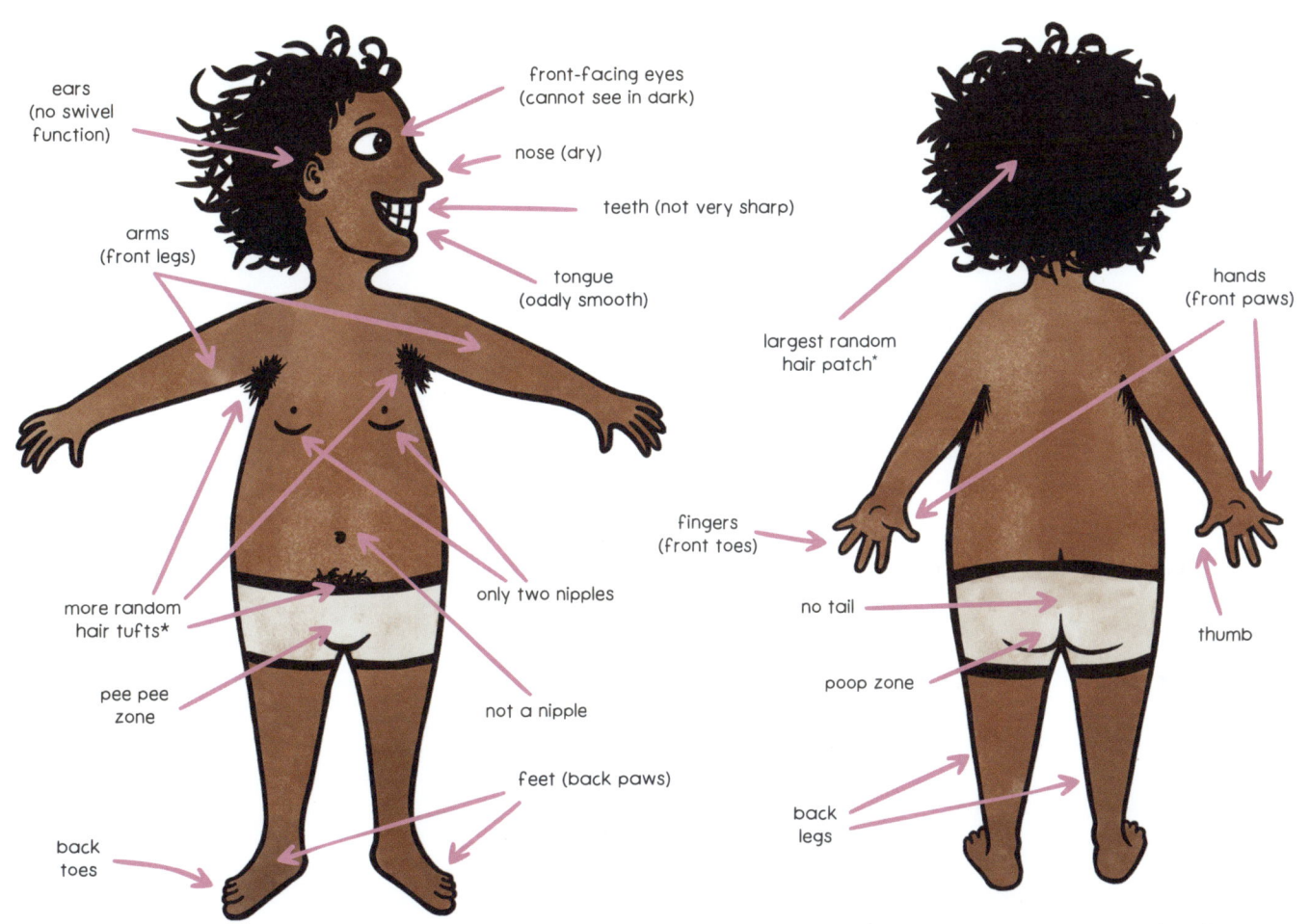

Left figure (front view) labels:
- ears (no swivel function)
- front-facing eyes (cannot see in dark)
- nose (dry)
- teeth (not very sharp)
- tongue (oddly smooth)
- arms (front legs)
- only two nipples
- more random hair tufts*
- not a nipple
- pee pee zone
- feet (back paws)
- back toes

Right figure (back view) labels:
- largest random hair patch*
- hands (front paws)
- fingers (front toes)
- no tail
- thumb
- poop zone
- back legs

*quantity may vary

Familiarising yourself with your human's body will help you understand some of their behaviours. For example, their eyes are poorly designed and cannot see in the dark. This is why your human may appear idiotic late at night, as seemingly obvious items can become real obstacles for them. Humans can be quite clumsy when it's light out, too, probably because their balance sucks. Hey, you'd be clumsy too if you were missing a tail.

Note that your human has only two nipples. Nobody is sure why, and nobody really cares. There is a strange hole in their bellies, which is definitely NOT a nipple. This crevice is mysterious and creepy as hell, so you'd be well-advised to keep your distance. Yes, we have it too, but ours is buried under fur and therefore not creepy.

bone structure

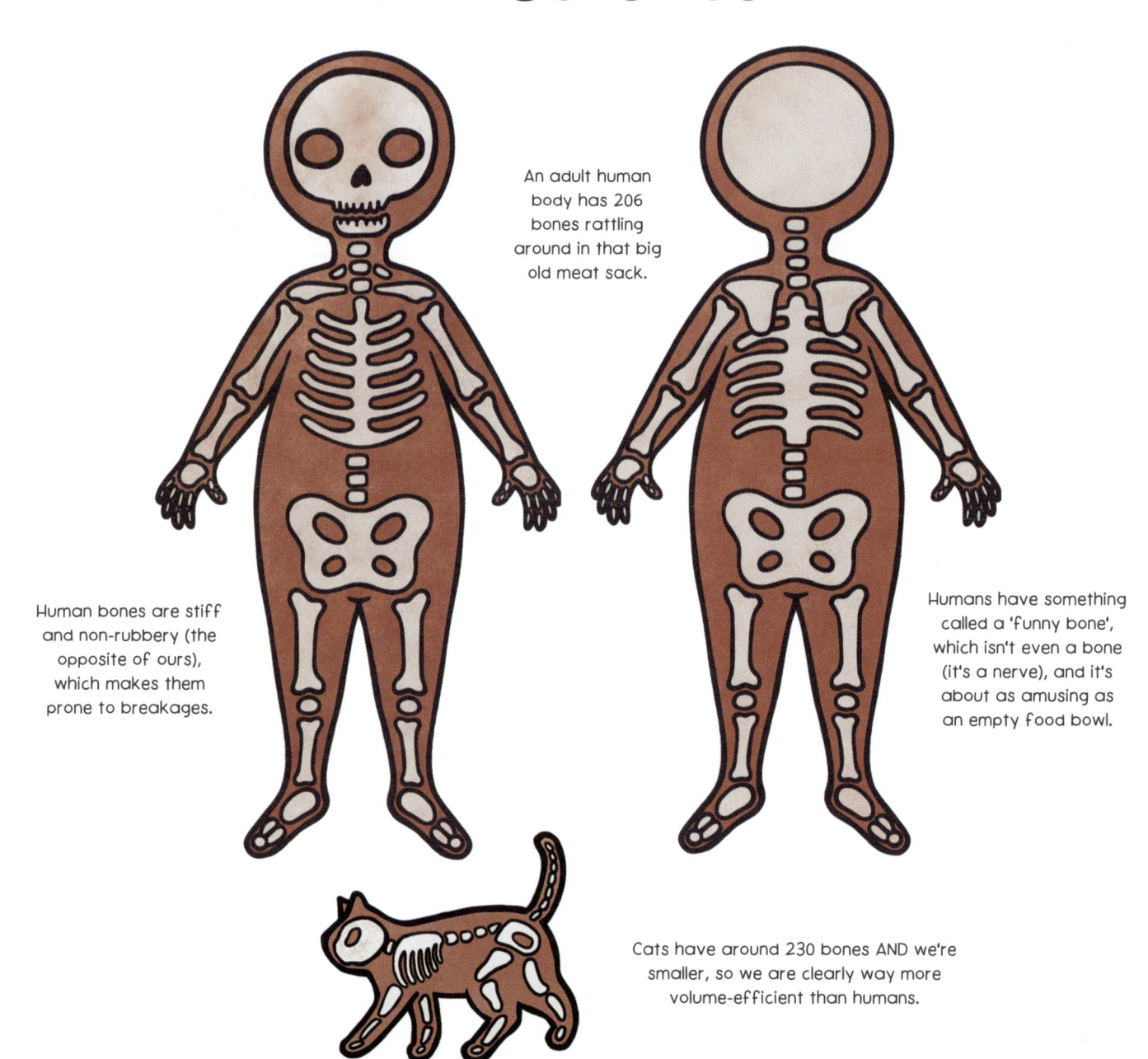

An adult human body has 206 bones rattling around in that big old meat sack.

Human bones are stiff and non-rubbery (the opposite of ours), which makes them prone to breakages.

Humans have something called a 'funny bone', which isn't even a bone (it's a nerve), and it's about as amusing as an empty food bowl.

Cats have around 230 bones AND we're smaller, so we are clearly way more volume-efficient than humans.

faults, outages & breakdowns
what to do when your human is unwell

Believe it or not, humans get sick. Of course they do – look at the bodies they've been dealt!

However, when your human is sick, you are under no obligation to perform any maintenance, make any adjustments, or administer any medications. That's on them. If they love you, they'll take care of themselves and not be so selfish as to make you worry for your own livelihood.

The average human takes way more medicine than we do. Yours may take some once in a while, short-term or long-term. Again, that's pretty much their business and you don't need to concern yourself with the details.

When a human gets sick, their performance and service to you will suffer. If you want your human to get back to work quickly, there are things you can do to help ...

fend off rogue tissues

offer comfort and practical support

teach the importance of hygiene

apply snuggles as needed

65

is your human normal?
a fair comparison chart

From time to time you will question yourself as a person-parent. This is beyond normal, and the fact that you even care shows you're doing a great job! There is much to learn, and you're not expected to know it all straight away. It's a journey of learning and discovery!

In this section of the book, we will delve into each of the following human experiences in great detail, but you can refer back to this **Quick Reference Guide** as a helpful resource whenever your human does something weird (which will be often).

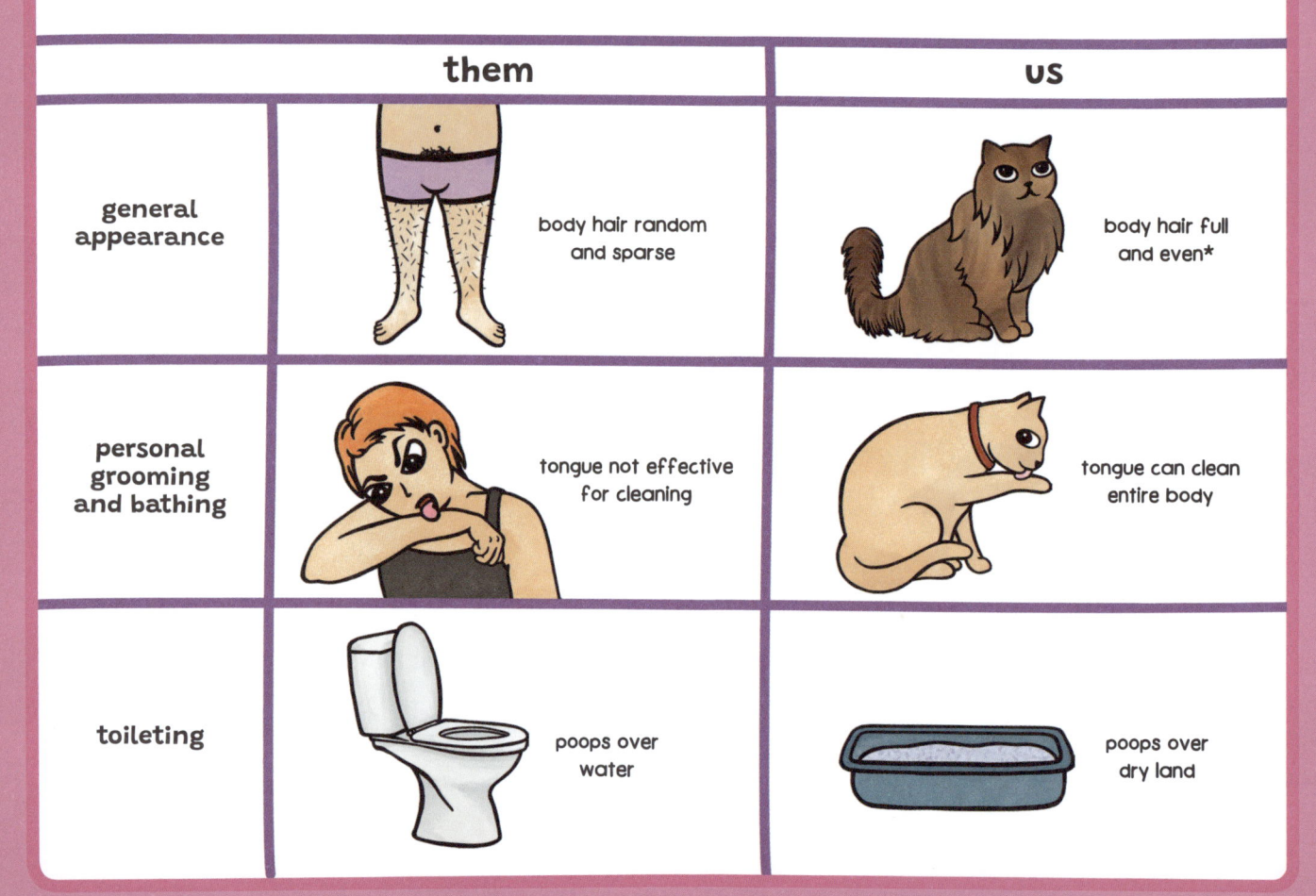

	them	us
general appearance	body hair random and sparse	body hair full and even*
personal grooming and bathing	tongue not effective for cleaning	tongue can clean entire body
toileting	poops over water	poops over dry land

*obviously does not apply to hairless cats

	them	us
fashion/ keeping warm	artificial layering, analogue temperature control	natural coverage, shedding auto-regulates body temperature
sleeping	6–8 h/night, confined to one spot	18 h/day, free to sleep around
eating	uses infinite dishes and cutlery	uses 1–2 bowls, 3 max
socialising	constant need for companionship and validation from peers	can take it or leave it
entertainment	magical screens, weird customs	window channels live 24/7

67

so your human has disrobed

why is this happening?

The most common reason a human will disrobe is to take a bath or shower. Watching your human shower is a spectator sport not for the faint-hearted, not only due to the confronting nudity but also the risk of splashback. Audience participation is STRONGLY DISCOURAGED. Same goes for baths. Sure, bubbles look like a great load of fun until you're in up to your neck fighting for your lives in their deep dark underbelly, consciousness flickering, light flashing from bright to dark as you gasp for air and then dart wildly from corner to corner of some slippery new porcelain realm like a lubed-up pinball on a hot winning streak.

Some humans find it unnerving to have an audience while they shower, yet will stare rudely at you while you bathe your own bunghole. (Some of them even take photos! Creeps.)

In these situations it is important to remember that you are the boss. Do not let them intimidate you. If you really do enjoy watching your human bathe and intend on making it a regular activity, one way you can gently prepare your human for viewership is by supervising them on the toilet every day.

remain calm

Seeing a human naked for the first time can be quite shocking – even traumatising, for some. Humans will get naked for a variety of reasons, and it is always a jarring experience that no amount of psyching up can prepare you for.

Humans have surprisingly little body hair, and the hair they do manage to grow appears in weird tufts on random sections of their body. This is clearly a design flaw and unfortunately there is nothing that can be done about it. You can try covering the bald patches yourself, or yacking up hairballs on these areas, but tricks like these have limited effectiveness and are usually a waste of time.

Some humans will grow hair on their legs, chest and/or back, but it's usually a pretty pathetic turnout of weak follicles and thin strands that are never quite up to the job. Some humans will grow a mane on their face in an attempt to emulate the mighty lion, but this mane is not very soft and they often get food stuck in it (which is something you can definitely help with).

This is why humans wear clothes. To their credit, they seem to do an ok job of covering themselves every single day. If your human is constantly naked, especially in winter months, that's when you should begin to worry.

what to do if you see your human naked

	reason for nudity	appropriate reaction
🛁	to immerse themselves in a body of water, such as a shower, bath or pool	Stay FAR away from said body of water. Seriously. Just leave them to it. They'll be fine. Stare awkwardly from a safe distance if you must.
zzZ	to sleep comfortably	Try to keep a sheet or blanket between you and your human. Use good judgement, depending on how cold it is and how open-minded you are.
🏃	in rapid transit from one room to another	Do whatever it takes to trip them over. It's always worth it and never gets old.
(o)(o)	to show another (usually also naked) human their body and compare parts	Stare at the other human. Do not leave. Do not break eye contact.
🍾xxx	as a side effect of consuming alcohol	Judge your human harshly. Show clear disdain. They'll pretend they don't care. They do.
⚽	to disrupt a ball game	Disown human. Keep ball.
🐱	to pretend to be a cat	Be offended. You may test them with The Signal* and some obscure feline trivia if you suspect foul play, but DO NOT encourage them.
#?!@	general buffoonery	Set clear boundaries by biting them. Make sure you stick to biting the tufted hairy areas of their weird body.

*If you're a cat, you know what The Signal is, so why are you reading this? Don't be weird.

analysis: human vs feline

	human	feline
nose	• large and prominent • dry (and sometimes crusty) • 5-6 million olfactory receptors means a mediocre sense of smell • considerable snot production • really only there for decoration and backup respiratory purposes.	• petite and cute as hell • glistens with a dewy glow • 50-80 million olfactory receptors make for a wicked sense of smell • not actually very snotty • serves many functions, can even be used for socialising!
ears	• hearing range of 20 Hz-20 kHz • zero swivel, no movement besides the odd wiggle (rare) • weird shape helps locate the direction of sounds • plentiful wax supply.	• hearing range of 48 Hz-85 kHz • sick swivel function - up to 180° • each ear can move individually • specialised design for precise localisation • modest wax supply.
eyes	• shape: round or a bit oval • round pupil that adjusts in size • can see 10 million colours! Ooft! • can't see at night • dodgy vision can be corrected with glasses.	• shape: almond (beautiful) • vertical slit pupil for light control • sick night and low-light vision • can detect movement • nobody knows if we need glasses or how we would even wear them.
tongue	• shape: broad and flat • flexible, muscular structure • subtle texture thanks to tiny bumps called taste buds • can detect five tastes: sweet, sour, salty, bitter and umami • mainly used for talking and eating.	• shape: narrow and long • rough texture courtesy of tiny, backward-facing spines • detects mostly salty and umami flavours (What the hell is sweet? Surely we're not missing much) • used for grooming and eating.

body & skill comparison

	human	feline
paws	• front paws are called hands and have five 'fingers' each, including a weird one called a 'thumb' • back paws are called 'feet' and have five toes each • claws or 'nails' do not retract for some reason, not even manually.	• five toes per front paw and four toes per back paw • adorable shock-absorbing beans cushion the underside of each paw • no thumbs (except polydactyl cats) • convenient auto-retractable claws.
brain	• big and bulky: 15 cm (6 in) • chonky: 1.3–1.4 kg (2.9–3.1 lb) • thinks too much, over-analyses • some commands bug out, e.g. `if (smart()==true) {speak;} else {shut up;}` seldom works.	• compact size: 5 cm (2 in) • lightweight and aerodynamic: 25–30 g (0.88–1.06 oz) • specialised for survival – hunting and sensory processing • no space wasted on BS.
speed	• average running speed is around 10–15 km/h (6–9 mph) • super fit humans can reach 36–45 km/h (22–28 mph) • can run long distances.	• faster than the average human, hitting speeds of up to 48–50 km/h (30–31 mph) in short bursts • built to run short distances • who needs endurance when you can just get stuff done quickly?
jump	• pretty lame – average vertical jump is 0.3–0.6 m (1–2 ft) • can possibly jump max 2 m (6.5 ft) – with a run-up, mind you – if they train extensively for years and years, lol • hilarious to watch.	• excellent jumpers – typically up to 1.5–2 m (5–6.5 ft) • powerful back leg muscles mean impressive jump height from standing still – no run-ups needed! • impressive to watch.

> **DID YOU KNOW?** about 50% of cats are right-pawed, 40% are left-pawed, and 10% are legit ambidextrous ... ... but true ambidexterity isn't really a thing in humans – about 90% of them are right-handed, and 10% are left-handed.

personal grooming

The human body requires a lot of upkeep, and some take personal grooming more seriously than others. You should always encourage your human to express themselves. Let them groom what little pathetic tufts of hair they have into a style that makes them feel fancy.

Unfortunately, sometimes what makes one human feel fancy makes someone else gag. That someone could be you. If this happens, or if you see that your human just isn't taking care of themselves as they should, you can start licking their hair into shape on their behalf.

They may struggle and resist your help, but you didn't sign up to live with some grot who can't work a comb. It's obvious they need to be shown what to do and how to style.

Hopefully, if your human is smart, they'll get the hint and learn quickly. If not, simply keep grooming them, but beware of really long hairs. Cats have been known to begin a simple groom on their human, only to get three inches into a clump and be latched onto strands that never end. This can wreak havoc on your intestines, so try to avoid it.

human grooming tools

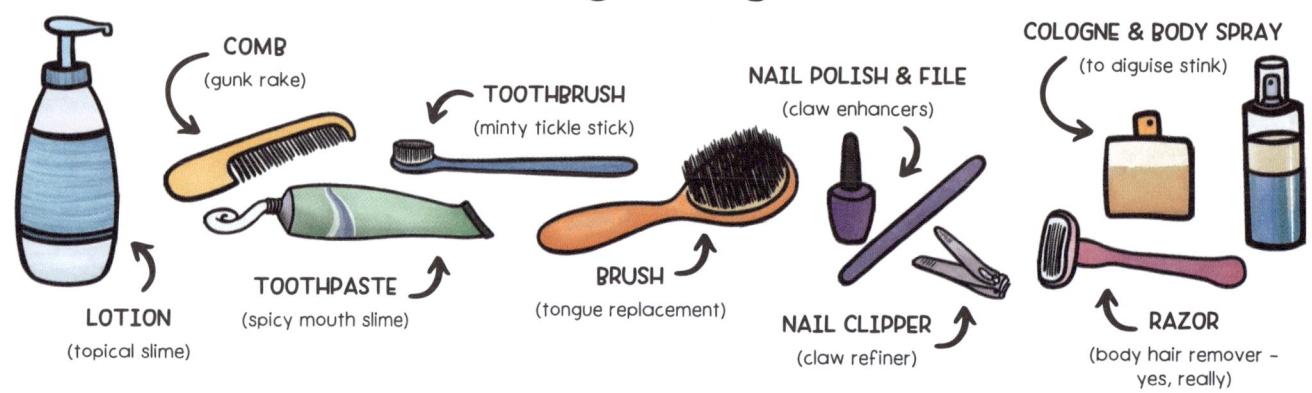

LOTION (topical slime)
COMB (gunk rake)
TOOTHPASTE (spicy mouth slime)
TOOTHBRUSH (minty tickle stick)
BRUSH (tongue replacement)
NAIL POLISH & FILE (claw enhancers)
NAIL CLIPPER (claw refiner)
COLOGNE & BODY SPRAY (to diguise stink)
RAZOR (body hair remover – yes, really)

feline grooming tools

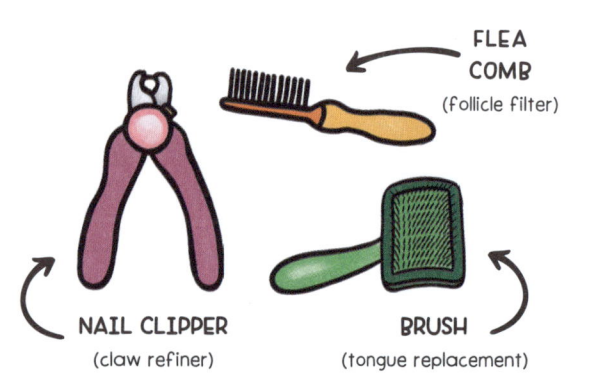

NAIL CLIPPER (claw refiner)
FLEA COMB (follicle filter)
BRUSH (tongue replacement)

returning the favour

A cute thing your human might like to do is brush your fur or clip your claws. They probably noticed you grooming them and thought it was a thing. Adorable!

Let them have at it. Humans need to feel like they're helping – it boosts their confidence and is probably good for their fine motor skills or something.

Sometimes they suck at it, like when they try to clip your claws and cut them too close to the quick and you feel a pain so excruciating you wonder if you're already dead. But if they stay close to the ends and only trim off the sharp bits, it can actually be quite nice, and stop your claws from catching on stuff.

Urge your human to start with something simple, like grooming you well with a decent brush. It feels delightful!

bathing

Humans can get pretty stinky, especially in the warmer months or after they've been doing their version of playing or zoomies. Humans do not have as many stench receptors as we do, but, to their credit, most of them seem to sense when it's time for a proper wash.

The average human doesn't really bathe on demand like we do, but they do need to clean themselves at least once a day if they are to continue living in society. If they are reclusive and never leave the house, they may think they can get away without a wash. But as their carer, and the one with the superior sense of smell, you know better.

The human tongue is smooth, not bristled, which explains why they do not bathe themselves in the normal manner, and tend to miss spots. Also, humans cannot yack up hairballs. They swallow them forever and who knows where they end up? Nobody.

For these reasons and more, your human will need the assistance of water in order to get a decent clean. Yes, that's right, water. The Devil's Venom. Satan's Elixir.

Do not be alarmed – human skin is impervious to water and they will not disintegrate or implode like cats would if large amounts of water were ever to engulf us. That's probably why humans are not terrified of water like we are. Good for them. Weirdos.

They will also need some kind of cleaning agent, such as soap, body wash and shampoo, to really get the gunk out. They really do have such inefficient bodies, so go easy on your human. It must be hard being such an inferior species.

Soap tastes gross. Do not eat it. In fact, what are you even doing near it? Generally you do not need to involve yourself in the undertaking of water-based bathing activities. If you are concerned about submersion or do not trust your human to wash every crevice, you may supervise. But know that if you do so, it may be at your peril …

DID YOU KNOW?

The average human can only lick approximately 20% of their own body! Yikes.

less effective/express options

Humans can bathe in a few different ways. While the most acceptable forms of human bathing are water-based, there are one or two less effective, short-term options for people on the go.

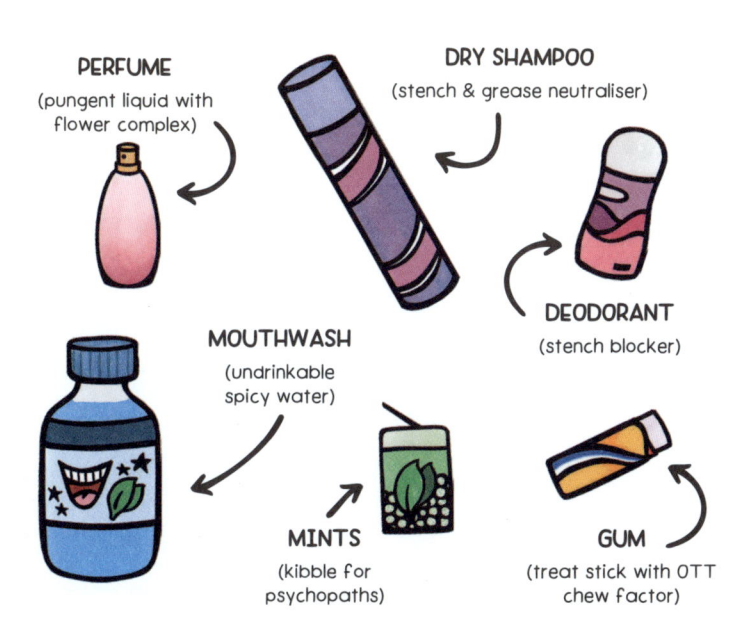

PERFUME
(pungent liquid with flower complex)

DRY SHAMPOO
(stench & grease neutraliser)

DEODORANT
(stench blocker)

MOUTHWASH
(undrinkable spicy water)

MINTS
(kibble for psychopaths)

GUM
(treat stick with OTT chew factor)

toileting

Shockingly, humans do not poop in a box or mound of dirt, instead opting to sit atop a BOWL OF WATER. So weird. What if it splashes? Did they ever think of that? Clearly not.

Many a cat has tried and failed to teach their person the classic Dig 'n' Bury method, but the human species is simply not intellectually advanced enough to get it. However, what they are capable of learning is how to serve you in your toileting journey.

Getting your human to become a master of all things poop is easy. Just follow these simple steps:

1. Immediately after eating, go directly to your litter box, or any spot you feel your litter box should be located.
2. Poop as per usual.
3. Kick litter as far as possible. The more area you cover with granules, the more fun it is for your human! If bits of your poo happen to fly out with it, all the better.
4. Leave the box with just a little smudge of poo on your paw, then walk around the house, adding a touch of class to boring plain surfaces with your subtle, elegant paw prints.
5. Watch your human scoop, sweep and clean. Look at the sheer joy on their face. Take a mental snapshot of this precious moment!

granules matter

To be fair, it may be a teensy bit unreasonable to expect scoop precision and proper litter box etiquette straight off the bat from someone who poops in a bowl of water and uses a roll of paper to clean it up, for fluff's sake.

Nevertheless, your human needs to know that granules matter. Teach them which kind you prefer, be it clumping, non-clumping, crystal, paper or wood. If they fill your commode with the wrong litter for your bum type, simply refuse and go do it somewhere else until they get it right. It's the only way they'll learn.*

when to throw paws

By law, you reserve the right to refuse your litter box and make alternative arrangements if one or more of the following events occurs:

- Your human doesn't regularly scoop up after you.
- They stiff you on the biweekly deep clean and instead keep pouring new litter on top of the soiled stuff.
- They stink-shame you (this includes making a face).
- You're stressed out by whatever fresh hell they've dropped on you this time (moving, new housemates, an especially handsy vet visit, loud noises, changes to your routine without prior consultation, generalised person-parenting stress, etc.).
- You find yourself sharing a single box with another cat. What disrespect is this?! Who does your human think they are? Demand one per cat plus a spare, damn it! Stage a poo coup!

*It's not strictly the only way. Would it kill them to pick up a book? Try leaving this one next to the toilet, open at this page.

the other side of the scooper

If you're having trouble educating your human, perhaps it's worth looking inward and thinking about what you're projecting. Are you being supportive of their own toileting journeys? Are you there for them, night or day, no matter the conditions, giving them moral support, watching them intently as they do their business, internally cheering them on?

Is your litter box within view of your human's toilet? If so, why not pop one out in solidarity next time they sit down? Humans learn by your actions, not your indistinguishable inner thoughts. Try leading by example and the rest will follow.

Of course, if traditional litter really isn't your thing, you can try other options. Nobody is asking you to hover over a splashy porcelain canal to do your business, but you should know that it is possible – many cats have used human toilets and lived to tell the tale. Most of them say they don't even miss the burying impulse after a while. Hey, no pressure. It's there if you want to give it a try.

If you really have to dig and cover, some more discreet places you might like to drop some dank nugs could be potted plants, garden beds, piles of dirt/leaves or a large box of sand.

keeping warm

lasagne, but not as you know it ...

It's no secret that humans have a pathetic amount of natural coverage. So far, the best idea they've come up with to stay warm is enrobing themselves with layers upon layers of garments or 'clothing'. On any given day, your human will essentially, voluntarily, become a big, gangly, colourful fabric lasagne! And they'll just walk around like that! It's wild.

If you think about it, though, this system is not such a terrible idea. When the weather warms up, a human will regulate their temperature manually by removing one or more layers. Inversely, they will reverse this process when they feel cold. Humans will do this instinctively, though they may sometimes gravitate towards you for additional warmth. If for any reason your human fails to adjust their clothing to the current climate, they run the risk of being uncomfortable, or worse – looking moronic, which in turn reflects poorly on you.

the cave of wonders

One area of the house you may take a while to set paw in is the infamous 'wardrobe'. A wardrobe, or closet, is a magical and sometimes scary world hidden behind closed doors. It holds all manner of secret surprises – some fabulous, some sort of ok, and some very, very, VERY bad. It's also a pretty good spot for a stealth-poo hideaway.

As you make your way through the hanging suits and gowns, breathe in the many scents of your human's cloth layers and picture where they've been. You may notice that a few of these clothing items are not to your liking – whether it be the colour, the texture or simply a weird vibe it gives you. It's imperative that you filter out this garbage as soon as possible to save your human from further embarrassment. That's just good parenting right there.

> Some humans prefer to store their clothing in a pile on the floor.
>
> This is called a 'floordrobe' and it's a great place to nap!

fashion vs fur

Anything humans can do, cats can do better. Except wearing clothes.

If you are a hairless cat, a tailored jumper probably won't look too bad, and will probably serve you well. A non-irritating fur replacement will not only keep you warm, but also help you perfect a bang-on impression of a dorky-ass human.

If you already have fur, you'll quickly learn that any piece of clothing you adorn will be nothing more than an uncomfortable obstacle between you and your motor skills. Worse than clothes are things like sunglasses and hats, which will only make you more uncomfortable, and cover up all the glorious things that make you a cat.

Of course, we can all understand why humans would want to cover up. But you, dear cat, have nothing to be ashamed of.

styling your human

out with the old

You see, before you came along, your human was probably just throwing on any old thing and hoping for the best. Now that you're in charge, it's time to start rebuilding their image.

It's in your best interests for your human to project confidence and sophistication. You want them to look good enough to be taken seriously, but not so distracting that they can't hide in the bushes if they need to. If you find anything in your person's wardrobe that does not fit this bill, promptly shred it to pieces and/or pee on it.

adding personal touches

While you'll probably decide quickly which items you want to shred or pee on, there may be a few decent pieces you can salvage and add your sparkle to. What is sparkle, you ask? It's fur. Your fur is the sparkle.

lending your expertise

To give the gift of style to your deserving human, try this fun exercise. Go through each piece of clothing, one by one, and ask yourself: 'Does this item of clothing conjure feelings marginally warmer than indifference?' If yes, put it on the **SHED** pile. If no, banish it to the **SHRED** pile. Easy-peasy. The rest is pretty self-explanatory – just don't get the piles mixed up.

If you're too good for piles, you can easily shed fur all over your human's clothes while they're wearing them, or while they're getting ready to go out. Some humans will be so keen for you to work your magic that they'll actually lay their clothes right out on the bed for you!

Shredding clothes to pieces is a slightly more delicate operation. It should be handled respectfully, with dignity, in the privacy of your alone time while your human is out of the house. This ensures that their surprised and delighted screams don't hurt your precious, sensitive ears.

The look you want to achieve here is a distressed version of the 'Nobody Knows I'm Hairless' meets 'Grocery Hunter Chic' aesthetic.

sleeping

night night

You will notice that your person rarely sleeps during the day. Many humans wait until the sun is well and truly out of the picture before surrendering to the sweet release of slumber. This is because they can't see in the dark, so they have to do the bulk of their looking around during the day.

Don't worry – your human has absolutely no idea what they're missing, so there's really no point in them being awake at night. You don't need them up in your business. That's your 'me' time.

Being a person-parent is tiring, especially if yours has kept you up all day (like so many newly adopted humans do). Some so-called 'experts' will tell you to 'sleep when your human sleeps'. The thing to remember here is that anyone who says this is well and truly out of their gourd, and would benefit from a firm swat with a litter-soiled paw.

dedicated sleep zone

There's not a lot of variety in a human's sleep location – they'll almost always pass out in the exact same spot. Humans come with specially designed beds, which are not only comfortable and large enough to hold at least one full-sized adult, but will also accommodate several cats.

Humans like to layer their beds with countless sheets, blankets and pillows to keep them warm – kind of like a nest – to compensate for their lack of body hair. These means that a human's bed, while embarrassingly overdressed, makes for an absolutely incredible hiding spot – see 'human bedding: where do you fit in?' (page 81).

alternative arrangements

If you find a human sleeping somewhere besides their designated bed, it is unlikely to be intentional. Such places as the bathroom floor or shower are clearly not designed for a human's awkward and gangly, hairless body. The couch, however, remains a mystery. It's unclear what this thing's deal is exactly, but there are cats looking into it.

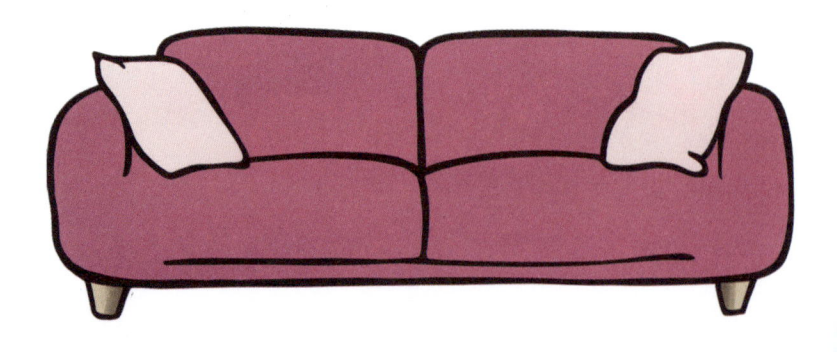

distinctive sleep attire

Humans appear to change their clothes for the specific purpose of going to bed, and will shy away from wearing these same outfits outside the home. Sleep clothes, or 'pyjamas' as they are known, appear to have some sort of sacred significance.

Some humans will opt for a long, flowing gown as their sleep garment, while others prefer a sort of glorified underwear blend. There are humans who, understandably, find clothing uncomfortable and will therefore sleep wearing nothing at all.

fascinating bedtime rituals

Unlike us, a human cannot simply realise they are tired and fall asleep. They have a whole litany of tasks they need to complete before they can make Zs happen.

Teeth-brushing appears to be protocol, as does face-washing and urination. Showering or even submerging oneself in a bathtub can be considered acceptable pre-sleep practices, though many humans opt for a wash in the morning when they wake up, as well as further urination.

limited duration

The majority of adult humans can only rack up an average of 6-8 hours of sleep per day, which, frankly, is pretty pathetic compared to our 16-20.

Freshly born humans can sleep a lot longer than grown ones - 14-17 hours. So, from this nugget of information we can safely deduce that humans are born robust and powerful, and will slowly lose their strength over time.

> Your deep-sleeping human will require something shrill, demanding and unrelenting to wake them up every morning ... but if you're busy, consider outsourcing that task to one of these helpful breakfast assistants.

common sleeping positions

Humans only have four primary sleeping positions, as opposed to our 53 billion.*

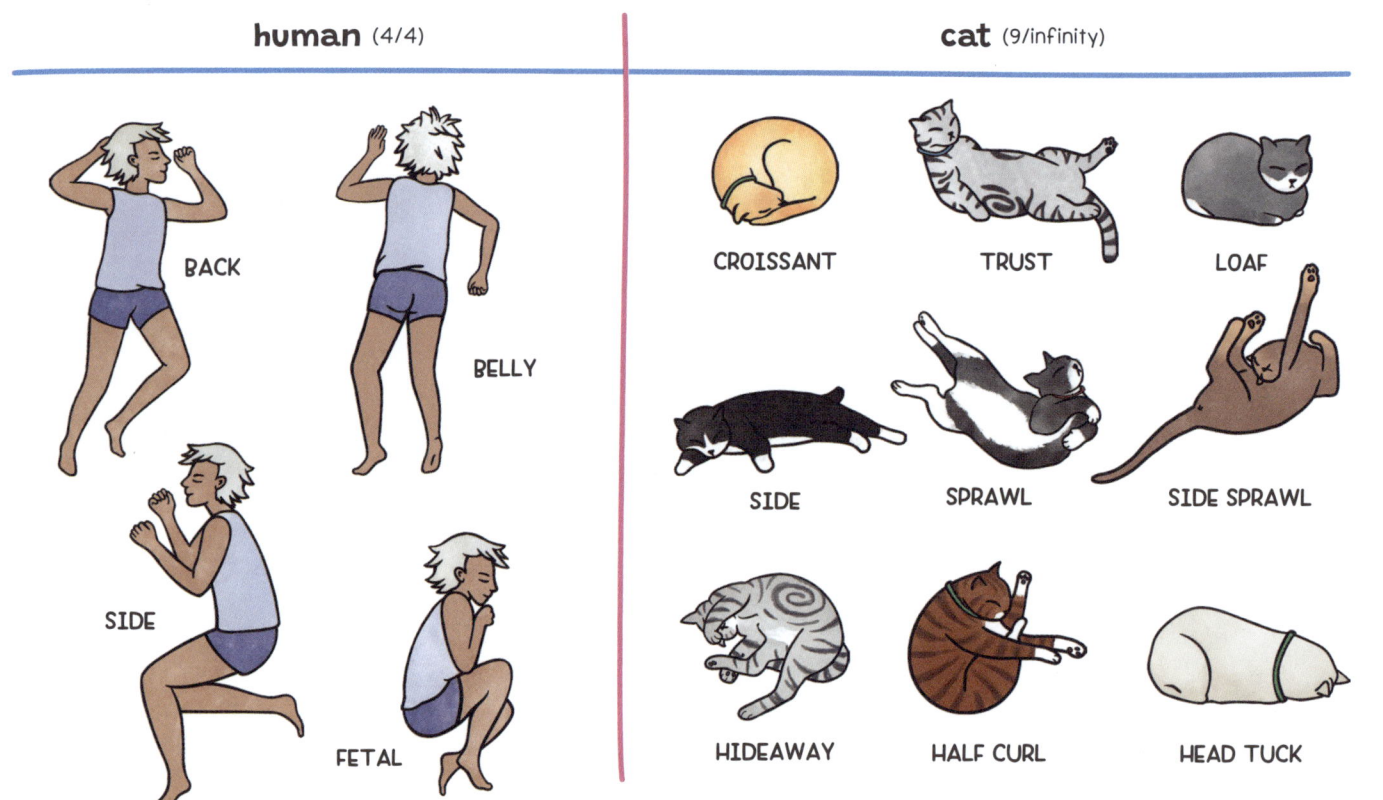

human (4/4) | cat (9/infinity)

human: BACK, BELLY, SIDE, FETAL

cat: CROISSANT, TRUST, LOAF, SIDE, SPRAWL, SIDE SPRAWL, HIDEAWAY, HALF CURL, HEAD TUCK

*by modest estimate

let's talk about toes real quick

If you train your human well, you won't have many responsibilities. But one job you will have – and must take VERY seriously – is keeping close guard of your sleeping human's toes.

While in a deep state of rest, most of your human's body will be completely motionless and covered up. Seeing this as a golden opportunity, one, some or all of your human's toes will take their chance to break loose of the rest of the muscular system and become their own separate entities. They come alive with great vigour and are extremely mobile.

These demonic digits will expertly shimmy their way out from under the covers. They can't go very far (they're still attached to the feet) but that's not the point. They deserve to be punished, and that's where your swift left jab comes in, with a side of sole-claw! Biting is optional.

human bedding: where do you fit in?

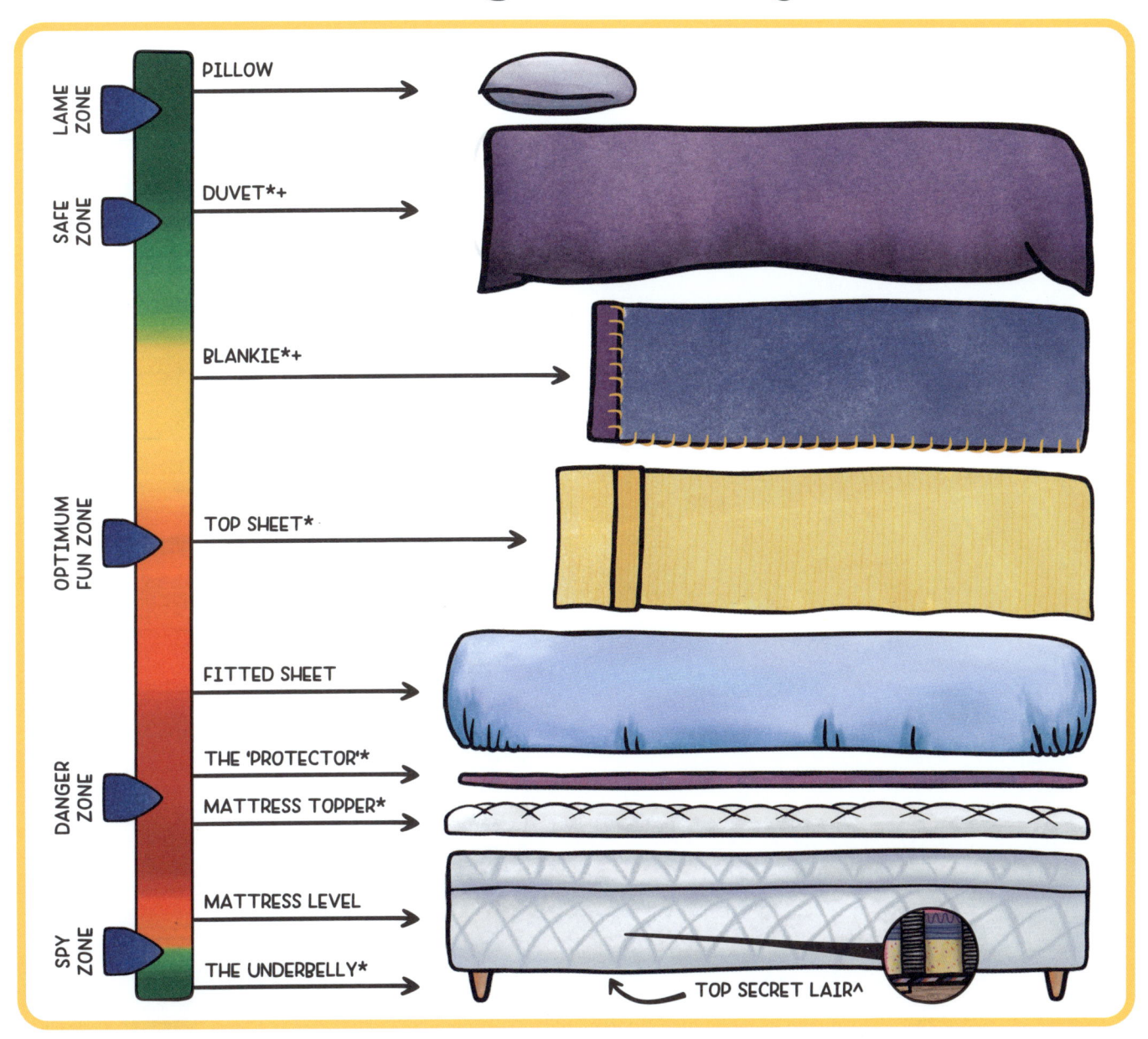

LAME ZONE	PILLOW	
SAFE ZONE	DUVET*+	
	BLANKIE*+	
OPTIMUM FUN ZONE	TOP SHEET*	
	FITTED SHEET	
DANGER ZONE	THE 'PROTECTOR'*	
	MATTRESS TOPPER*	
	MATTRESS LEVEL	
SPY ZONE	THE UNDERBELLY*	← TOP SECRET LAIR^

*may not appear in all beds as some humans find this level unnecessary
+availability subject to weather/season
^extremely rare

eating

what does a human eat?

Give minimal care to what your human is eating. Definitely make it your business to sniff each meal and paw at it if necessary, but don't stress too much if you smell something questionable. If your human is alive, that's good enough, and it means you're doing a fine job. Don't put so much pressure on yourself!

It is not advisable to get too deeply involved with your human's dietary choices. Obviously, if you like your human, you want them to eat well and stay well, but beware the human who talks about their diet nonstop.

If you hear the word 'keto', run in the opposite direction and don't come back until they're done talking (this may take a while). Be sure to do this every time and be consistent. It's the only way they'll learn. If you are too tired to run, just fart and leave the room. They'll get the message eventually.

how do humans find food?

For the most part, despite their suboptimal bodies, humans seem to be ok at hunting. When they leave the house each day, this is where they go – to get food. Sometimes they are successful, and you will see them return with their findings all lumped together in some sort of bag (cute!). Reward them by glancing in their direction, or not biting them.

Other times, they'll come back empty-handed, and you should take these opportunities to make your disappointment clear.

when to intervene

If you notice your human coming back too often without any food, you may need to take matters into your own paws. You can do this by bringing them a mouse or a bird (preferably dead since they are clearly incapable of killing effectively) or, failing this, a large bug.

A nice thing to do is to put the kill on their pillow as they sleep – that way they'll wake up to a delicious breakfast! Hopefully, seeing your expert catch will demonstrate what they could be doing differently, and inspire them to try harder next time. Note their excited screams. Repeat this process until you get the desired result.

'variety' is a thing. ha.

Unlike us cats, humans don't seem to understand the benefits of eating the exact same thing every single day.

If you or I changed foods or even flavours all the time, our bellies would not be pleased. There'd be diarrhoea for days and voms off the chain. Gross.

Humans, however, have complex digestive systems and seem to be able to consume all manner of crap without hurling it up (most of the time). Some humans are naturally healthy, whereas others may have a penchant for 'junk food'. This is why it's important to err on the side of caution when stealing from their plates – you never really know where their food has been or what it will do to you.

how much is too much?

As cats, we generally eat only two meals – breakfast and dinner. Humans, however, are sitting down to stuff their faces three or more times a day! Is it because they need more fuel in their big gangly bodies? Is it because they don't have fur to keep themselves warm? Is it because their lame human food is so unsatisfying that they need to try new stuff all the time in the hope they'll find something decent? Probably all of the above.

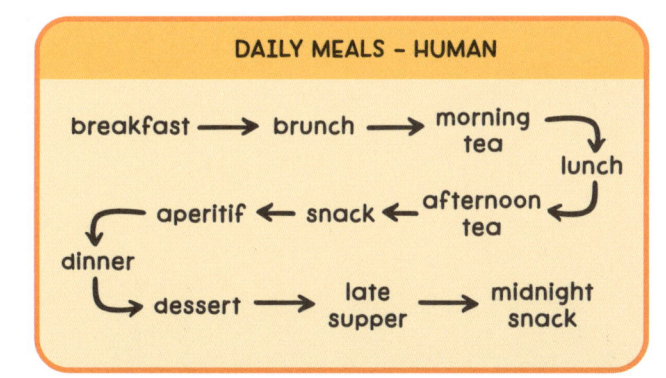

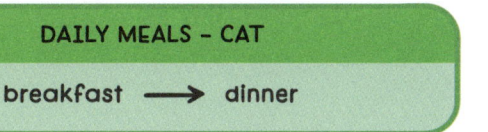

DAILY MEALS - HUMAN
breakfast → brunch → morning tea → lunch → afternoon tea → snack → aperitif → dinner → dessert → late supper → midnight snack

DAILY MEALS - CAT
breakfast → dinner

stealing vs yoinking

Humans are not allowed to eat cat food. At least, that's what we tell them so we get more for ourselves. So far, as a collective species, we've managed to fool them, and they're generally pretty good at staying off the kibble. However, wet or fresh food can be deceptive and it takes a keen feline eye to tell the difference.

Understandably, humans often get confused, so it's your job to educate them. If you see a piece of fish or chicken on your human's plate, you should confiscate it immediately by way of swift consumption. That's right – take one for the team.

Your human may refer to this as 'stealing' and will probably object. If this happens, grab said food in your mouth and leg it to another room or place where your human cannot reach.

The correct term is actually 'yoinking'. Yoinking is when something is rightfully yours (or should be yours for the sake of protecting someone or satisfying your own wants) but is in someone else's possession, so you've gotta just go up and yoink it. Stealing is when it's something you really deserve. The difference is subtle but important.

Gulp this forbidden morsel down before your human can ingest it and possibly make themselves more confused. Imagine if they were to eat it and like it – they may think it's ok to eat cat food, thus leaving your precious dinner bowl susceptible to infiltration.

socialising

one, two, pee in a shoe

While the majority of cats who adopt a human (or humans) are happy to go it alone, it's not uncommon for a couple, throuple or even a whole clowder of cats to adopt the same person at the same time. Why? You see, some humans are needier than others, so often more than one cat is required to assist with their abundance of issues.

In most cases, an adoption team will be siblings, close friends or cage mates, which means there'll be very little drama. Sometimes, though, it's just you and some random puss(es) you've never met, who just happened to be cosmically assigned to the same person.

Will you get along? Will you share the same values? Will you be able to co-parent without scratching each other's eyes out? Nobody knows for sure. Just try to remember that you share a common goal: training a human to serve the greater feline species. Sharing the load means you'll have less work to do, and you can take out any frustrations by peeing in things like bags or shoes without anyone immediately knowing it was you.

sharing is scaring

A food bowl is made for one head to fit in, not two, and certainly not three. There should be plenty of food to go around, but if you're a slow eater or the type to graze and leave leftovers in your bowl, you're in for a flying trip to reality junction.

In a shared environment, unattended food is fair game. You snooze, you lose. Literally.

Litter is much the same. Ideally you'll have your own poop box, one per cat, plus a bonus one if your human is educated. Litter boxes are interchangeable, and you're welcome to poop in whichever one is cleanest at any given time. But what you don't want is to be hovering over the granules with another cat at the same time. That's just weird, even more so if you make eye contact.

when in doubt, hiss it out

Human adoption is sometimes done in phases. A human may have been adopted by one cat, then later present as needing more support. You may be adopting your human by way of reinforcement, either because the other cat(s) were not entirely capable, or because your human is a freaking doozy.

Of course, with staggered adoption comes inevitable tension. No one wants to feel like they can't handle things on their own, nor does one adopt a human thinking they won't be the one in charge forever.

Rest assured there will be a customary hissing ceremony, which can last anywhere from a few days to a few months. This procedure should automatically sort things out, but if not, try 3 am fight club.

CLAWS OUT!
CAT vs CAT

FIGHT CLUB
TONIGHT 3AM

dogs and other animals

Dogs are interesting housemates. They are not your responsibility. They are not your human's primary caregivers. They're just ... there. Society expects you not to get along with them, but this is a total myth. Of course you can happily coexist with a dog, rabbit, horse, cow or any other animal your human drags home. Sure, these folks may look weird and have far fewer brain cells than you, but they can be trained, so don't shy away from bossing them around. At the very least, they can be used for warmth on cold nights (if you can get past the smell).

undesirable house guests

Humans are social creatures by nature. They need other humans around. You don't have to like the people your person brings home, but you do have to tolerate them to a degree, and try to appear supportive.

You are your human's best judge of character, so anyone you don't like should be an immediate red flag. Warn your human, but don't nag – it's very unbecoming. If they're smart they'll read the signs and pick up on your disapproval fairly quickly.

If not, they might live in denial for a while, but hopefully clarity will prevail sooner rather than later and they'll come to their senses. This is when they'll speak the five greatest words a person-parent can ever hear: 'My cat was right about you.'

love and let love

Pretty much every cat wants their human(s) to be happy and find love. Obviously it would be great if all of that love was reserved for you, but there can be room for others, too.

If you like someone your human has brought home, let them know by the traditional method of ignoring them profusely as they slowly earn your trust. If they are worthy of your human, they'll work for your approval. If they stick around long enough, you may just decide to adopt them too.

In some cases you may grow to like this secondary human even more than your first-adopted. In this instance, upgrade to the newer human, pledge your undying loyalty, and leave no survivors. Sorry, not sorry.

weird human customs and traditions

Being a human is likely very boring, which is why yours may choose to spice things up and entertain themselves by taking part in seasonal customs and traditions. Most of these events will occur once a year, though some humans will keep the party going way past what is considered cute. Beware of people who just don't know when to quit, as you could be hearing jingle bells long after you've chased Santa's intruding ass back up the chimney (though that could just be your collar).

You may or may not be expected to get involved in every single hostile home takeover. However, you will have to accept that decorations will go up, other humans will drop in, and things are gonna get pretty weird for a hot minute or two. The best thing you can do (if you don't fancy joining in, that is), is find a nice quiet spot out of reach, loaf yourself up all cosy and snug, and try not to get too upset about everything. Don't worry, it'll be over soon enough.

the exchanging of gifts

A human will do this thing where they get all stressed-out hunting for a random object of varying crappiness, wrapping it in special paper (which they don't even roll around on first), and then presenting it as a gift to another human. This custom seems to be a bit like mousing, only with no clear defining purpose.

The human who receives the gift will make a face of joy (either genuine or forced) and give thanks of fluctuating sincerity. The giver will then explain the gift in great detail, beg the recipient for reassurance that they like it, and then offer to take it back.

The gift will sometimes be accompanied by a piece of card which the recipient will stare at in silence for a good eight seconds before either smiling or bursting into tears. So weird.

off-key singing and fire food

For some reason, roughly once a year, your human will shove a stick in your food and light it on fire. Why? The motive for this remains unclear, but it appears to be some sort of bizarre ritual designed to summon a new meal order, perhaps altering the dish in some way.

All humans present will stand around warbling a poorly synchronised off-key chant, at times clapping their hands together. Then you can either bat the fire with a paw (not recommended), or a gust of wind will just come out of nowhere and the fire will disappear. It's wild.

After this is done, the magic stick is removed. You are then expected to sniff this either cursed or enchanted food and advise whether or not the spell worked. Note that the food in your bowl may appear different from your usual meal - this is the effect of the spell. Sniff it. If it's enchanted, you'll want to eat it. If the food is cursed, you'll walk away or simply stare at your human in disgust. Uncanny.

Unfortunately, there seems to be a breakdown in this ritual somewhere, because no matter whether you liked the food or hated it, your meals will go back to normal the very next day, and everyone will act like nothing happened. These people are out of their gourds.

a tree inside the house

Sometimes humans will come to their senses and realise it's not all about them. The fog of neediness will clear and they'll see you not just as their primary caregiver, but as a noble cat who might like to be at one with nature. In short, they'll want to start giving back.

Whether you're an outdoor, indoor or hybrid cat, your human will opt for practicality and bring a tree inside the house for you. Yes, a tree! Sure, it's indecorously abstract and a little uncouth, especially given that in most cases it isn't even a real tree. But you can't deny that a tree at this proximity is delightfully convenient, not to mention incredibly thoughtful.

In case it wasn't clear by now that your human is doing their best to please you, they'll go one step further and decorate this tree-shaped celebration of plastic with an array of gaudy objects. Upon closer inspection, these objects are actually toys for you to take down and destroy.

Your human will make a game of it, pretending to be mad at you and then rebuilding the tree, replacing decorations so you can go again. This continues until they get bored, at which point the tree will disappear, only to return a year later covered in dust. Fascinating.

black cat appreciation day feat. pumpkins

There is an interesting tradition wherein a selection of humans will spontaneously gather to celebrate black cats. For black cats, it's a lovely sentiment indeed. However, if you're not a black cat it can feel a tad creepy – and, quite frankly, RUDE – as you're left feeling overlooked while your human puts on this embarrassing display of obsession.

The black cat celebration may feature backup acts like skeletons, bats, witches and pumpkins. But perhaps the creepiest part about this yearly tradition is when humans dress in attire that is stranger than usual, sometimes even resembling gigantic cats. They say imitation is the highest form of flattery, but humans can never quite seem to get our proportions right.

Decide for yourself how you feel about all this. Just be aware there is a chance you may be forced to dress up too.

DID YOU KNOW?

Pumpkin is VERY good for you when served properly.* It contains fibre to help you poop, loads of water to keep you hydrated, and it can help you feel full without adding extra calories!

So, dig in if you dare to diet, which I do not because personally I'm not that into pumpkins.

*Stick to cooked or canned pumpkin without any salt, sugars, spices or other additives. Don't eat raw pumpkin, pumpkin seeds or pumpkin pie filling – it could take you to vom town.

part five

making your human the best they can be

obedience training

setting intentions

JFK* once said, 'Ask not what you can do for your human, but what your human can do for you', and boy was he onto something.

When you first adopt someone, you're allowed to baby them a little. They'll mess up and need your guidance, and that's ok. You might even mess up too (but probably not). You're both new to this and mistakes are bound to be made (by them, not you – you're perfect).

What JFK was clearly on about back there, and the crucial thing a few slow cats might forget, is that the human's true purpose in life is to serve the feline. Denying your human (or yourself) this opportunity would be a direct attack on everyone's natural instincts. That's just plain cruel.

So, before you go any further, you need to make the conscious decision to heed the words of JFK forever and ever, and NOT to be a jerk about this.

Did you do it? Did you heed? Ok great. Now, read on so you can learn how to crack the whip and kick your human into gear already.

above: JFK (artist's impression)

establishing routines

Some cats choose to be more rigid than others when training their humans, and how firm (or soft) you want to be is a personal parenting choice (actually, your softness is more of a diet thing).

Some cats say that a strict daily schedule is necessary for mental health, as it aides in reducing anxiety for both parties (see suggested daily schedules, page 107).

Others say the opposite: that being too inflexible causes more anxiety and sends the human into complete overwhelm.

The third, and oldest, line of thought concedes that some humans just aren't the sharpest claws in the paw, in which case it's best to operate on a vigorous pendulum of low expectations and incessant meowing.

The graph on the right shows where you should be putting your energy when dealing with a difficult human.

Here we can clearly see that in order to counteract any deficiencies in your human's intellect, your meowing should intensify as the situation becomes more dire.

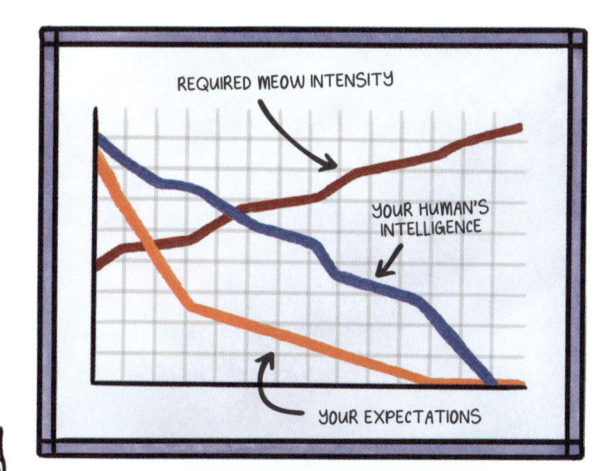

Did you know? Calculating your human's meow response time is the only reliable way to measure their IQ.

*Jasper the Fearless Korat

the five agreements

When you adopted your human, they made an unspoken, unwritten and unbeknownst-to-them pact with nobody in particular, which was to blindly follow The Five Agreements, no questions asked.

Each 'agreement' refers to one essential aspect of your daily life and, with your guidance, your human will learn the importance and delicate intricacies of each and every one.

Over the next several pages you'll be given instructions of varying coherence on how to properly implement and enforce said five:

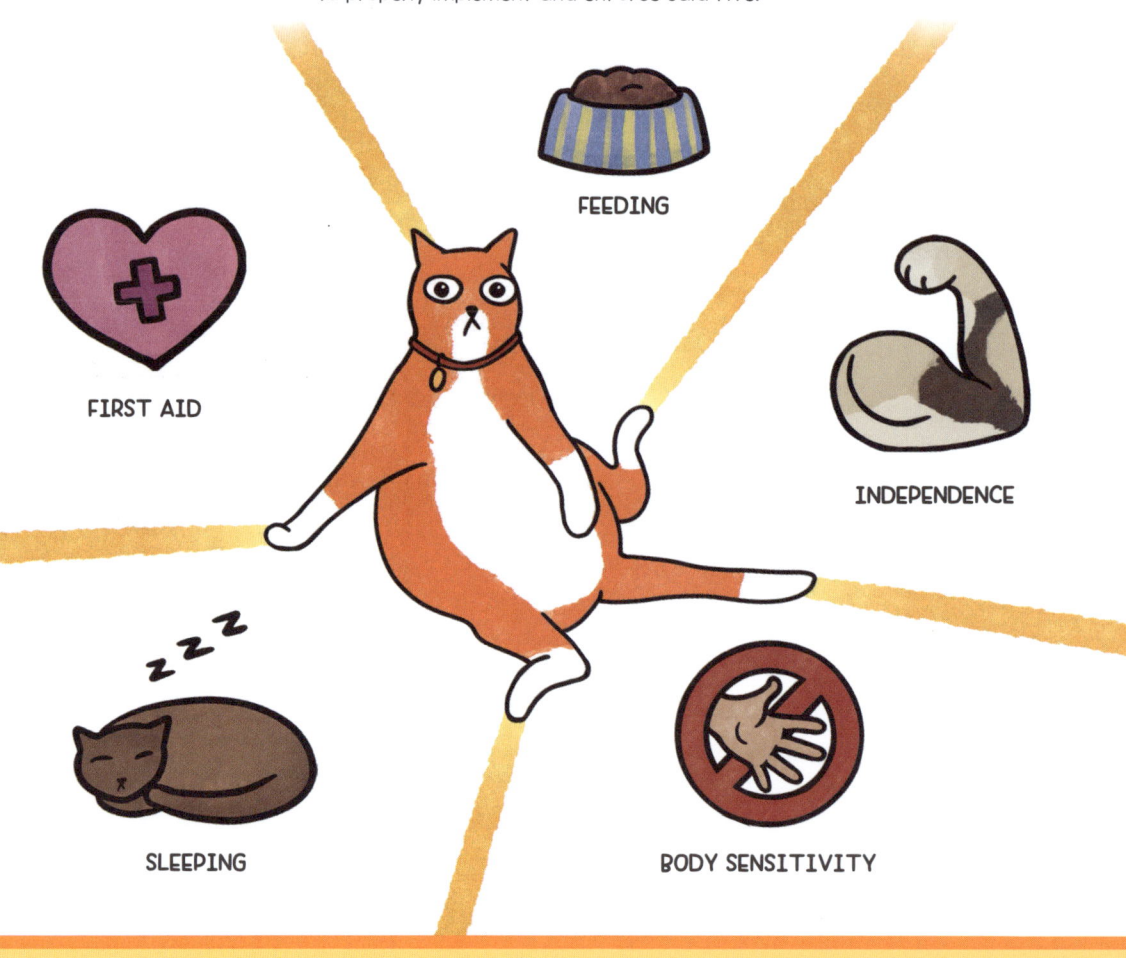

FEEDING

FIRST AID

INDEPENDENCE

SLEEPING

BODY SENSITIVITY

agreement 1: feeding
eating well and on time

timing is everything

Training your human to feed you on time takes dedication, consistency and an internal body clock of oscillating accuracy.

Your human should learn to feed you twice a day, as a matter of high importance. It's imperative they show up on time - no exceptions - and do the job efficiently so you can get to work inhaling your bickies.

The key points are getting the timing right, and putting the food in the bowl all by themselves. Sure, it's annoying waiting for them to do it. They'll likely be slow, make a mess and get the presentation all wrong.

Fight the temptation to shove your paw in and do it for them, because they simply won't learn this way. Oh, and don't even think about hunting for your own food - it would shatter their confidence and they may never feed you again. Leave DIY hunting for emergencies only.

Some humans have higher standards and stronger work ethics than others. Those who are dedicated to perfection have discovered they can outsource dinner and breakfast duties to an automatic feeder.

Yes, there is some controversy surrounding these machines - on one paw, they feed you on time, every time, and they don't sit there talking nonsense while they do it.

On another paw, they won't teach your human the value of sticking to a routine, which is basically the pinnacle of their training structure. It's suggested you wait until your human is an expert in manual feeding and you're out of kittenhood before accepting kibble from a robot.

wet vs dry

As the old saying goes, 'Kibble for breakfast makes you strong, wet food for dinner lives you long.' Ok, so that's not a real saying, and what does 'lives you long' even mean? Who cares. It's true, regardless, so train your human to remember it.

You may prefer dry kibble or you may prefer wet food, though it's advisable to get your human comfortable with feeding you both. Dry kibble is good for your dental health (you do NOT want to go down the route of having your human try to brush your teeth – see below), and wet food can help keep you hydrated. Sure, you can mix them together if you're DTF (down to fuse), but it's not always a pleasure. Beware the stale remix, where a human tries to add wet food to yesterday's stale kibble dregs. Grot.

Having said that, if you're missing a bunch of teeth, you might want to just stick to wet food and no kibble, or even just broth so you don't embarrass yourself. There's nothing worse than looking foolish in front of your subordinate(s).

I firmly believe that wet food and dry food should never associate with one another outside the stomach! But don't let my correct opinions ruin your gruel ...

DECONSTRUCTED/ WET-DRY SEPARATION

NOTHIN' BUT WET

STALE REMIX FEAT. DAY-OLD BICKIES

WET + DRY MIXED TOGETHER

If you're curious about brushing your teeth, simply make your way to the bathroom, locate your human's toothbrush and have a little nibble on it. Eww, what is that? Is that mint? Gross. No thanks.

BUT watch what happens when you turn around and rub that same toothbrush on your back end instead! Ooft! So satisfying!

You're welcome.

treats

Treats are a crucial training tool. If you can train your human to give you treats on command, you've probably reached Peak House-cat Status.

Sure, too many treats might make you a big fat fatty bum-bum and cause you all sorts of health problems and costly vet visits. Sure, people will berate your human, accuse them of animal abuse, and try to get you to un-adopt them. Sure, you might develop a taste only for treats and refuse to eat your regular food ever again, but hey! YOLX9!!

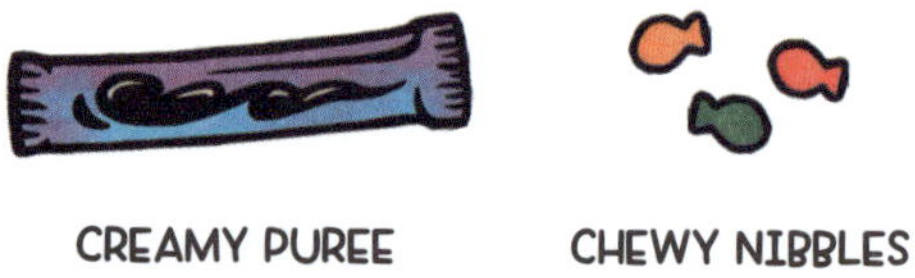

CREAMY PUREE

CHEWY NIBBLES

get to know your packaging

WET FOOD MINI CAN

WET FOOD SACHET

WET FOOD CAN

WET FOOD POUCH

UNMARKED KIBBLE DISPENSER

KIBBLE BOX

KIBBLE BAG

quality assurance

When it comes to feeding you, your human will instinctively take this job seriously and therefore assume they know what's best. But think about it – have you ever seen a human eat cat food? Hopefully no. And we want to keep it that way.

Obviously, the main reason humans don't eat cat food is that they respect us, and they respect (most) boundaries. But this also means that humans have no idea what cat food really tastes like. Sucks to be them.

So, as part of their service to you they'll usually find the tins with the prettiest looking cats on the package (don't get jealous, they're not as pretty as you) or foods that have ingredients they like – and therefore think we'll like. Adorable. However, a gorgeous puss and promises of flavour do not necessarily live up to the hype once that can is tapped.

It's important to nip this quality thing in the bud. With each new meal, carry out the official feline three-step appraisal:

1. taste-test
2. pick the best
3. vom the rest.

setting a precedent

The number one mistake a lot of cats make when training a human is being too liberal with positive reinforcement. Some cats will eat whatever is on offer, just to encourage their hopeful human. Big mistake. Huge.

Yes, yes, it's very impressive that your human has learnt how to feed you, but that doesn't mean you have to chug down whatever old slop they spoon out! This small and seemingly generous gesture can actually set a dangerous precedent, and dictate the tone of your dining experiences for years to come. Do you really want to be eating low-grade 'mixed meat flavour' (whatever that means) for the rest of your nine lives? Do you? DO YOU?

too little too late?

If it's already been a while and you're worried you're trapped in a doomed menu, don't despair. You can still train your human to feed you well – it will just take a little extra work on your part. It's never too late to take a swift paw to your bowl and yeet your dinner far and wide. It's your right as boss, after all.

food tasting basics

The three main food groups are big-ass birds (also known as poultry), fish and meat. The fourth is human food, but we talked about that already. The fifth, less popular food group, is Mystery Slop. Nobody knows what that is, and nobody wants to know what that is, so best not to look too far into it. The sixth is dog food, which you'd be well-advised to stay away from. Seriously, don't eat dog food. It does look a bit like cat food and you'd be forgiven for thinking it's fine, but it's really not – it's hard on your delicate stomach and it's not going to do your bunghole any favours. Just ... no.

Fish is generally the most popular cat food, as it's something our ancestors would have eaten in the wild without much trouble. It's not so simple to catch a big-ass chicken and cook it up in a fancy stew when you don't have any thumbs, now is it? Fish is also a better choice because it's slimy and pungent and there are rarely any feathers to get stuck in your teeth. Watch out for bones, though.

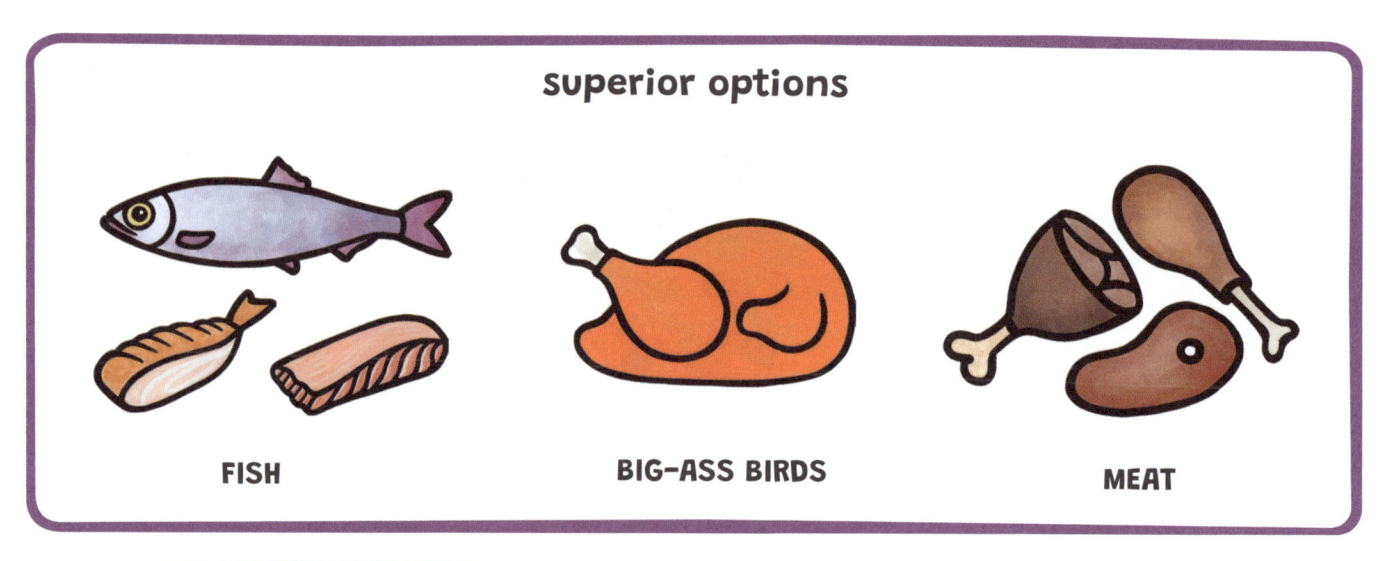

superior options

FISH **BIG-ASS BIRDS** **MEAT**

hit & miss

HUMAN FOOD **MYSTERY SLOP** **DOG FOOD**

the more refined palette

Believe it or not, there are different types of fish in the world, and some of those will end up being cat food. Thankfully, cat food-quality fish are all edible, but you might prefer tuna over salmon, or cod over sea bass, for example. If you can't tell the difference, don't worry – not everyone can be fancy and dignified. If your human can't tell the difference, consider their level of intelligence and subpar sense of smell.

Luckily, lots of foods have little pictures or icons, and are usually colour-coded according to flavour. If your human can't read, is colourblind, and can't tell a salmon icon from a tuna icon, you're screwed. Go for chicken.

The main thing is knowing what you like, and the only way to find that out is by tasting every possible food available. It is absolutely key that your human is intensely involved in this process. They must live and breathe your meals, waking at the crack of dawn with their first thought being your breakfast.

If you're serious about extending your flavour selection, your human must train hard, and be suitably disciplined when they make mistakes. They must not rest until they have perfected Advanced Recipe Selection, Can-Opening Techniques and Optimum Feeding Conditions that have been carefully curated to suit your way of life.

what's that icon?

- **BEEF**
- **TURKEY**
- **CHICKEN**
- **OCEAN FISH/ TUNA**
- **LAMB**
- **DUCK**
- **UNDEFINED**
- **SALMON**

know your rights

You reserve the right to change your mind at any point and request a whole new revised menu without prior notice. It doesn't matter if your human has stocked up for months in advance.

However, bear in mind that you may need to go hungry for a short amount of time as your human leaves to hunt and forage for something suitable. Stand (or sit) your ground. Humans need to feel challenged. They may seem confused or annoyed at first, maybe even downright pissed, but deep down they appreciate the sentiment.

the stand-off method

If you have rejected a meal, you may hear your human mutter the phrase, 'If they're hungry they'll eat it.' If this happens, do not be alarmed.

The No-Eat-No-Feed method is an old, tired, empty threat – your human is testing your boundaries. It's crucial you maintain your stance that the food is inedible and stay resolute. Do not give in to starvation tactics under any circumstances. You do not negotiate with terrorists. If you're really starving and they still won't budge, meow incessantly.

the false alarm

Sometimes your human will return from a grocery hunt with food for themselves in canned form. You will understandably mistake this for your own, because human food in a can is one of life's cruel and unnecessary jokes.

Canned goods cause all sorts of confusion, not only because they look the same as our staple meals, but because the pop-schlip sound of a ring-pull being yanked is pretty dang universal. Distinguishing the difference between a can of tomatoes and a deep-sea casserole opening is almost impossible.

It doesn't stop at cans, either. Is your bowl ceramic? Learn the exact note and pitch it makes when hit with a spoon. Is your kibble in a box? Prepare yourself for the absolute mind-melt that is breakfast cereal. Are your treats in foil wrapping? Good luck with that.

Not to be confused with the shake 'n' fake (page 101), detecting a false alarm requires sharp hearing, strong intuition, and the kind of expectation-free mindset that comes from extensive experience with chronic disappointment.

The only other way to really know for sure is to look at the label for either a picture of a cat, or one of the icons on page 95 – but even those can be misleading. We are all familiar with the urban legend about a Siamese who bolted down three flights of stairs at the sound of a spoon tapping on a can. He did his due diligence, saw a chicken icon and everything! What a rude shock he got when the food inside turned out to be an insult not only to cats everywhere, but also to minestrone.

diabolical design

Check out these examples of seemingly harmless packaging on a number of cat vs human products. Look how they are cleverly crafted to mess with your head. Unbelievable.

KIBBLE CRUNCH VS CEREAL MUNCH
It doesn't even make sense! Why does the corn have a face??

INSTANT FISH CREAM VS INSTANT CAFFEINE
50% chance of instant disappointment

EL GATO MEAL VS TOMATOES, PEELED
Is it food in a can? Or food in a can't?

human/cat crossover foods

Never forget that unlike your omnivorous dependent, you're a carnivore first and foremost. While meat should make up pretty much your entire diet, there are a select few foods that can be enjoyed by cats as well as humans. These foods aren't ever going to be your first choice by any stretch of the imagination, but it can be helpful to know what unknown treasures may be wasting away in your human's creel. After all, this person is working for you – why shouldn't you maximise your benefits?

> If you fancy sampling human food, make sure it's cooked and pureed. It must be totally free of added salt, sugars, spices or fats, lest you inelegantly disgorge. Nobody wants to see that.

> Hold up. It says here that you should always eat in *gasp* moderation? That can't be right ...

Safe-ish human foods to lick and/or nibble sometimes

- CARROTS
- PEAS
- PUMPKIN
- GREEN BEANS
- EGGS

disposing of unwanted food

If an unsolicited foreign morsel has appeared in your bowl and you've implemented the obligatory tap-sniff-lick protocol with negative results, you may want to dispose of it. In this situation it is advisable to weigh up the pros and cons of ousting said morsel before making any sudden moves:

PROS:
- it's gone
- no chance of it staying there and being avalanched by your next meal, leaving you to relive the experience.

CONS:
- human may see empty bowl, mistakenly assume you ate the offending scrap and liked it, then provide repeat serving(s) in future.

If you decide to go ahead with disposing of it yourself, best practice is to carry it to a secondary location where your human will see it and therefore determine that it was not well-received. Options include on their pillow, in their shoe, or on the floor next to your bowl where you can keep a close eye on its movements.

sharing food

You should never willingly share your food with anyone, especially not your human. Dogs will certainly give it the old kennel try, but you can easily stop them with the usual canine-eradication methods in your instinctive toolkit.

If there are other cats living in your house, they should bugger off and mind their own business, though you may choose to let them have at a few dregs after you're done.

The only time another cat might be justified in eating your food is if you are a very polite gentlecat, and a smaller, weaker cat (such as a feeble kitten) is starving nearby. Letting them go first to fill up their tiny belly is a modest yet generous sacrifice indeed. Be careful, though – if you keep letting that kitten cut in front of you, they'll slowly rob you of your protein source, leaving YOU the weak and feeble one. See what they did there? Diabolical! And do you really think they're going to return the favour once the crumbs are on the other paw? Not a chance.

Moral of the story? Don't be fish-cally irresponsible.

agreement 2: independence
getting your human to leave you alone

The flip side of the mild fulfilment you get from person-parenting is that humans can be really, really, REALLY annoying at times. You've gotta have your downtime, lest you succumb to The Horrors™. Sure, it's nice to be needed, but do you really want to be waking up every nine hours to attend to a whiny human? Come on.

To teach a human to fend for themselves is to liberate yourself and become you again. You're more than just a person-parent – you're a cat first and foremost, and it's easy to forget that sometimes.

Independence training really only requires one word, said three times for effect (or better yet, not at all) …

IGNORE

IGNORE

IGNORE

… That's it!
Ok, that's not it. But it's mostly it.

the business of busyness

Keeping a human busy is a great way to get some peace. Their brains, while hefty and cumbersome, do not fully understand object permanence. Therefore, if they are distracted enough, it's almost as if you don't exist, which means they're off your back for once.

Humans are creatures of habit, not unlike us. But instead of simply popping over the fence for a quick kill when they're hungry, they prefer to do their hunting on specific days of the week. They usually leave and return at the same time each day, and they'll be gone for hours at a time. This is great news for you, and means you'll get some much-needed respite.

Some humans will do their hunting remotely, which is an impressive yet infuriating skill. Remote hunting means they don't leave the house and you're stuck with them. However, it can still function as an ok distraction if they are dedicated to their tasks.

It's important you support your human's hunting schedule. Walk them to the door in the morning as they leave, and greet them when they come home (if you're into that). If your human hunts from home, the object-permanence thing can become problematic, and if left too long they could neglect food service. Make sure your human remembers you exist by making them (and sometimes their hunting buddies) take regular breaks to look at your bunghole.

agreement 3: sleeping
training your human to respect rest

As a cat, you will sleep roughly 18 hours a day, so it's crucial you find (or create) several good locations that challenge your human and develop their problem-solving skills. By no means should you stick to the same nap spot every time – shake it up! Part of good person-parenthood is making your human (a) search for you, (b) freak out when they can't find you, and/or (c) trip over you.

A traditional nap spot will be tucked away from main traffic areas, and ideally high up so you can sleep-spy on your human and other household goings-on. That being said, there's much to be gained from sleeping in the middle of a busy hallway, on top of a handbag or on a vital staircase step.

Sure, some spots can present physical risks, but don't shy away from them. Humans need obstacles! Tripping over you once in a while puts their balance to the test. In addition to keeping them agile and limber, they get to practise apologising profusely and feeling bad. Play your cards right and they might even come grovelling with treats.

command zzz

If your human is regularly bothering you and you're not getting enough sleep, it could have serious consequences for everyone involved. Some humans may not understand how much sleep you really need, and wrongly assume that you are sick or injured. Ironically, the only injured one will be your human if they don't knock it off and give you some space. Fortunately, there is another solution: hide.

napping vs hiding

The difference between hiding and napping has a lot to do with intention. Going to a particular spot with the sole objective of napping is a deliberate choice known as 'conscious unconsciousness'. This can be shortened to 'Cons-Uncons', which sounds fun if you say it in a French accent (no disrespect to *les chats*).

The same goes for deliberately seeking out a hiding spot. You don't want to be found, but you intend to stay awake there, usually for the purpose of a game. This is called 'Fun Contrived Disguisement', which shortens to 'FuCoDis'. This one sounds more Italian than French though (no disrespect to *i gatti*) and doubles as something to say when you get sick of playing.

Where the lines get blurred between napping and hiding is in the timing and events that follow. See, napping can be a happy accident that comes as the result of a successful hide, but it doesn't usually work the other way around. The former will usually happen if the hiding spot is comfortable and warm, has an interesting texture, or is new to you. The latter would only happen if you genuinely didn't realise your chosen nap spot was inconspicuous.

hybrid locations for concealed snoozing

LINEN CUPBOARD
Tuck yourself in between the many layers of softness. If you do it right, even an open door will not expose you.

CAMO-PARGE
Anything the same colour as you will create an illusion of uniformity.

COUCH LINING
If your couch's undercarriage is not readily accessible, you may need to claw yourself an access point through a weak spot in the lining.

ye olde shake 'n' fake

Picture this: you're in a deep sleep, dreaming about adopting a young Harrison Ford, when you hear a bag of kibble rustling in the distance, or perhaps the tapping of a spoon on a can. It must be dinnertime, right? WRONG.

Your human has just lured you out of your cosy, warm nap spot. They even made you break into a light trot. And for what? A succulent bowl of LIES, that's what.

Yes, it's true: there is no food. This is all just an elaborate ruse to get you to pay attention to them, and it's called the Shake 'n' Fake.

If, by no fault of your own, you happen to fall for this trick, use it as an opportunity to educate! Help your human learn some damn respect – the rule is:

IF YOU SHAKE IT, YOU MAKE IT. No exceptions.

Forcing your human to feed you each time they lure you out is great practice for following through with commitments, and it teaches them the value of a kept promise. Plus, yay for bonus snacks! Your human will learn that if they want you to come to them when they call out to you, they MUST cough up the goods EVERY SINGLE TIME.

If your human won't comply, you are well within your rights to ignore them anytime you hear an unscheduled shake in future. You are allowed to hold this grudge forever.

agreement 4: body sensitivity

a touch of class

Newly adopted humans can have very little understanding or familiarity with the feline body. They will also be super excited to have been adopted, and may enthusiastically grab or squish parts of your body, inadvertently causing annoyance or even distress with their liberal affections.

If your human touches any of the red zones by accident, give them ample warning.

If they touch them on purpose and think it's funny, it's time to reassess your approach and establish stricter boundaries.

If they continue to touch the red zones repeatedly, even though you've made yourself water-fountain-ly clear, start making escape plans and/or plotting your human's demise.

getting yourself in the zone

Human bodies, on the other paw, do not have such strict and delicate boundaries. As you can see from the map (right), the entire human body is a free-for-all safe zone for you to sit on/jump on/dig your paws into with reckless abandon.

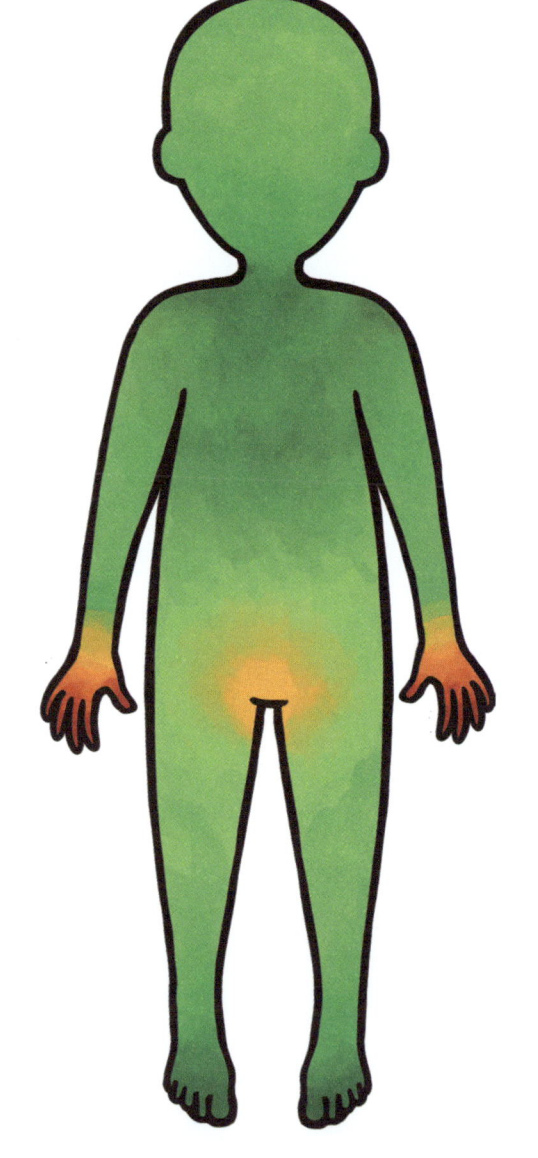

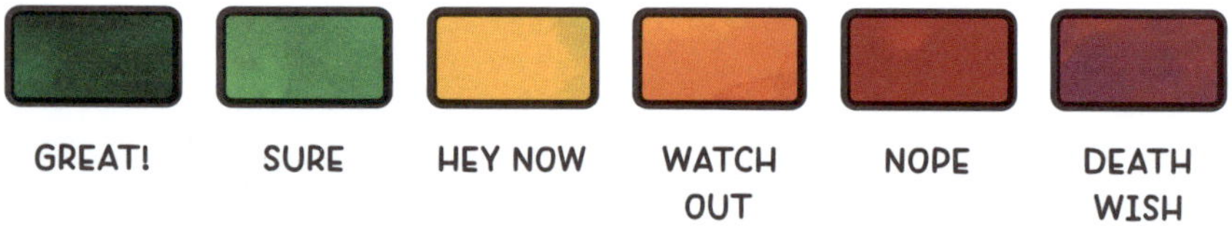

GREAT! | SURE | HEY NOW | WATCH OUT | NOPE | DEATH WISH

the great belly paradox

ways cats show love	where it goes horribly wrong	ways humans show love
head bumps not suffocating humans in their sleep despite countless opportunities to do so lap biscuits	**belly stuff**	kisses and cuddles, neck scritches using photos of you from every angle as the background on all devices weirdly specific, off-key serenades

decent exposure

As cats, the highest honour we can bestow upon a human is showing them our bellies. It's a beautiful gesture of pure trust! Humans, however, having been conditioned for centuries by belly-scratch loving, attention-seeking dogs, will automatically misinterpret this kind gesture as an invitation to take their grubby hands to your body and start furiously rubbing. Gross.

Therefore, if you expose your belly to a human and they rub it, they immediately obliterate your trust in them. Then, because you rightfully attack them for this, their trust in you is broken too. It's a vicious circle (depending on how vicious and/or circular you can be) and it needs to end. But how? To break this chain, you'll need to either:

a. stop trusting humans

b. put up with being belly-groped and live in shame

c. teach your human that your body belongs to you, and is not up for grabs, literally.

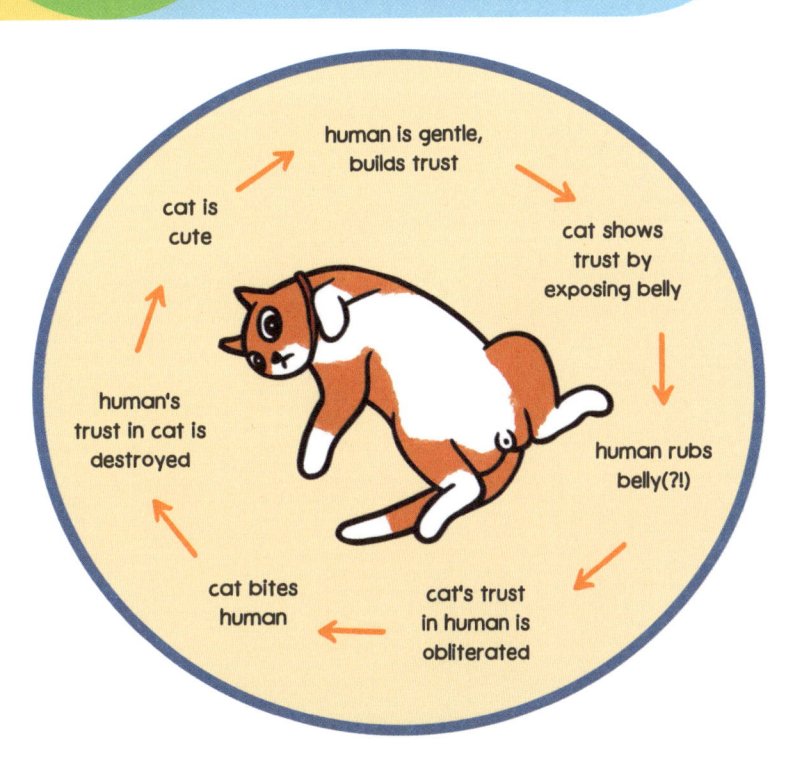

The cycle: cat is cute → human is gentle, builds trust → cat shows trust by exposing belly → human rubs belly(?!) → cat's trust in human is obliterated → cat bites human → human's trust in cat is destroyed → (back to start)

CONCLUSION:
Dogs have ruined humans for everyone. If and when you feel ready to expose yourself, proceed with caution.

agreement 5: first aid

in case of emergency

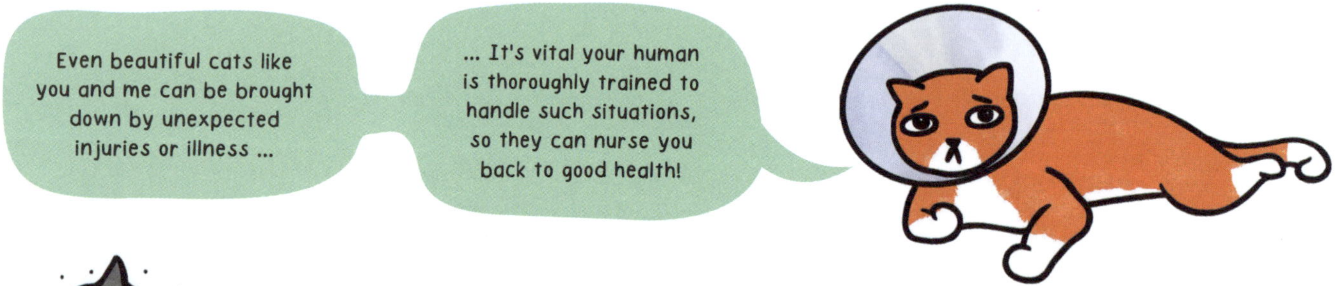

Even beautiful cats like you and me can be brought down by unexpected injuries or illness ...

... It's vital your human is thoroughly trained to handle such situations, so they can nurse you back to good health!

fleas

Did you go outside, have a wild time with another cat or two and then come home itchy? It could be fleas, you dirty pervert. Thankfully, your human can be trained to rid you of them at home with spot treatments, special flea collars or medicine. If your human doesn't take action, simply pass them your fleas. They won't be able to stand the itching for long.

the cone of shame

The Elizabethan Collar is just a fancy name to make you feel like a queen, when in reality you'll look like a novelty vacuum cleaner that can't clear a bowl. While wearing one, you cannot eat, drink or lick your gooseberries, hence this thing's REAL name, 'The Cone of Shame'. If you find yourself being neck-crowned with one of these bad boys, just try to be positive and enjoy the benefits: if you look up and sit still long enough, you can catch bugs in it. Or, at the very least, some dust or leaves.

dental health

Turning your mouth into a bacteria party can not only cause stank breath, it can also lead to all sorts of serious health issues throughout the rest of your body. Make sure your human knows that your teeth are precious. You can do this by biting them.

Keeping your teeth healthy is a huge deal, so make sure you're getting checked out regularly, and cleaning when necessary.

vet visits

Your human is responsible for keeping you healthy, but they're clearly no genius. Someone who is, though, is a strange breed of human called a VET (which stands for 'Very Eager with Thermometers'). These humans are OBSESSED with us on a whole other level.

A vet can check you out for all sorts of ailments, though you may not enjoy every interaction. Yes, they are supersmart, but they can get a little handsy. Also, as their name suggests, they have a bizarre fascination with thermometers – namely putting them in your bunghole. Weirdos. Just try to relax and remember you're safe – it's all in the name of good health. Probably.

medications

There will come a time in at least one of your lives when you'll have to swallow a pill of some sort. It won't be pleasant, it'll taste gross, and you'll hate it. But you have a human to take care of now, which means you need to survive. It's time to embrace modern medicine, because looking for vitamins in patches of grass and fending off predators with rapid-fire sneezing will only get you so far.

If your human is experimenting with giving you medications, there's a good chance a vet pressured them into it. In fact, your human probably won't be able to get their hands on any of the good stuff without a vet running interference.

Pills, also known as tablets, medicine, medications or meds, are a vile yet magical gift from the universe. They actually do way more good than harm, so try to keep an open mind.

Yes, they taste revolting. Yes, they feel horrendous going down your gullet. Yes, they can make you feel out of control for a hot minute. BUT they will also make you feel better in time, as long as you trust the process.

chewables

Medicine in chewy treat form is growing in popularity. While the taste is probably not exactly what you'd be hoping for, the effects are undeniable.

choosing the right approach

Of course, you reserve the right to choose nine lives of pain and suffering, but remember that medicine can make you better! It is not your enemy, despite appearances, smells and tastes. Thankfully, there are palatable ways to ingest medication, and more than a few methods you can choose to be drugged. Pick the one that's right for you and ride the wave, bro.

staying healthy

You already know how helpless humans can be on their own, so it's in their best interests – and yours – for you to live all nine of your lives at a glacial pace.

- Don't eat things you shouldn't. Stick to good quality cat food, nothing cooked with oil, salt, sugars or spices (see page 87).
- Take care of your teeth. If they hurt, get your human's attention by crying when you eat, or simply not eating at all.
- Get regular health checks.
- Keep your weight under control. It's easy to gorge, but if your portions are too large, have some self-control and just walk away.

quiz: which type of person-parent are you?

Now that you've learnt all about adopting a human, it's time to figure out what your parenting style will be. Answer the following questions and tally your scores to determine your fate.

START HERE

1. **Which of the following describes you best?**
   a. strong physique, firm paws, sturdy tail.
   b. classic good looks, clean fur, unassuming tail.
   c. slightly dishevelled, a tooth missing, crooked tail.

2. **Do you have time for nonsense?**
   a. no. Absolutely not.
   b. not really, but I'll allow it every now and then.
   c. all of my time is exclusively dedicated to nonsense.

3. **How far are you willing to go for the wellbeing of your adopted human?**
   a. to the ends of the earth – I'll do whatever it takes!
   b. to the ends of the street – I'll do my fair share but I'm not making any wild promises.
   c. to the ends of my paws – anything out of reach is just too much effort.

4. **Your human has put the wrong food in your bowl. How do you react?**
   a. meow angrily. Flip the bowl. Drop an immediate floor poo.
   b. sniff what they provided, look up at them with bemusement, and wait for a reasonable explanation.
   c. uhhh, hold up. Other cats get fed? Like, food? In a bowl?

5. **It's well past wake-up time and your human is still sleeping. What do you do?**
   a. execute an emergency hairball. Nothing gets a human to their feet faster than the sound of you throwing up.
   b. gently paw their face and nuzzle them awake.
   c. fart and/or go back to sleep.

Tally your scores. If you answered ...

mostly a — you're probably **the stickler**
a super strict authoritarian, completely unyielding.

mostly b — you're probably **the peacekeeper**
a fair and reasonable person-parent, fairly structured, flexible when necessary.

mostly c — you're probably **the low-baller**
a mild-mannered, mostly chill caregiver with loose morals and even looser bowels.

suggested daily schedules

THE STICKLER

06:00
Wake-up call via shrill meow and face slaps. No snooze allowance.

06:01
Serve portion-controlled bickies in stainless steel bowl situated at precise kitchen floor coordinates, no spillage.

06:05
Present at latrine, scoop fresh poop, deep clean and refill, meticulously comb granules like sacred Zen garden.

06:06
At ease.

17:59
One-minute dinner warning.

18:00
Serve one sachet of Fishy Yum-Yums in left compartment of dual-selection dish, portion-controlled bickies in right. Dish to be situated at precise kitchen floor coordinates, no spillage.

18:07
Present at latrine, scoop fresh poop, meticulously comb granules.

18:10
Supervise public display of admiration with Mr CuddleBear.

18:30
Assume position, prepare for lap biscuits.

21:00
Lights out.

THE PEACEKEEPER

7–7:30 am
Wake-up call via snuggles and head bumps, which repeat on snooze.

7:30 am
Pour unmeasured bickies in bowl, just whatever you think is about right.

7:45–8:00 am
Scoop fresh poop. Refill or clean if necessary.

8:00 am
Free time.

5:30 pm
Snuggle time.

6–6:30 pm
Serve one sachet of Fishy Yum-Yums with a side of bickies.

6:45 pm
Scoop fresh poop. Refill or clean if necessary.

7:00 pm
Sit next to me on the couch while I take a relaxing bath.

7:30 pm
Snuggle time.

anywhere from 9:00 pm – 11:00 pm
Bedtime.

THE LOW-BALLER

between 9 am & 12 pm
Wake-up purrs.

some time after wake-up
Crack the kibble bag open, or put it somewhere I can knock it over and graze at my leisure.

after breakfast
Leave me to my own devices.

5:30–6 pm
Play the 'Guess Where I Pooped' game.

6–6:30 pm
Leave dirty dishes on kitchen counter for open sampling.

7 pm
Watch me lick my bunghole.

7:30 pm
Toleration time.

anywhere from 11 pm – 2 am
Pass out on couch, drop a selection of crumbs on own chest for sampling.

not long after that
How do you like this foot in your mouth?

a while after that
Here's a mouse I caught for you.

a bit after that
Whoa, your hair tastes like that spot behind the garbage bin.

troubleshooting
for when things go wrong

problem	possible cause	solution
Human is not responding to voice commands.	Ears are broken.	Meow loudly into ear canal.
Human is watching something you don't approve of on TV.	Needs mature guidance.	Sit on remote and manipulate stomach muscles until channel changes or TV turns off.
Human is sleeping with toes exposed.	Toes are attempting to escape (bad).	Attack offending toes and detain in custody (see page 80).
Human keeps getting up from chair.	Thinks they are busy and important.	Immobilise by sitting on lap.
Human will not get up from couch.	Legs don't work.	Bite to check.
Human has not returned home at usual time.	• Sucks at hunting. • Is ashamed of bad hunt.	• Continue to wait. • Grow exponentially pissed with each passing hour.
Food bowl looks like it has food in it but is actually empty.	Human has been fooled by optical illusion.	Summon human, command freshening bowl-shake magic trick.
Human appears to be vomiting.	Human is unwell.	• Sit on back while hunched over. • Vomit on floor in solidarity.
Human has pulled your tail or touched you in a sensitive area without consent.	Human is unhinged.	• Release warning growl to conjure Satan. • Hiss. • Execute swift left jab.
Human has groped your primordial pouch.	Human is confused or uneducated.	Initiate spring-action body clamp.

problem	possible cause	solution
Human's eyes appear to be leaking water.	Human is sad.	Get close enough to offer comfort, but not so close to be mistaken for a tissue.
Human shook food but did not pour.	Human is a massive jerk.	Remember this forever, and vow never to come again when called, even in case of emergencies.
Human appears to be locked out of house.	Human has forgotten how to use door.	• Meow instructions loudly from other side of door. • Pull faces from window.
Human has an attitude and tells you to 'get a job and start pulling your weight'.	Human is going through obnoxious developmental phase.	Do nothing even harder.
Friend of human comes to visit several days in a row.	Friend wants to poach your human and adopt them for themselves.	• Pee in friend's shoes. • Offer friend blood-drawing services. • Fake an injury, framing friend for animal abuse.
Human has been sitting in front of computer for too long.	• Has fallen under concentration spell. • Has forgotten how to live.	Break spell with forceful smooch.
Multiple people have appeared on human's computer screen.	They heard great things about your bunghole and have assembled to see it.	Give the people what they want.
Human is lying in bed with eyes closed, emitting some sort of high-intensity throat purr.	Human body experiencing technical difficulties.	Jump on chest to restart.
Human has been sitting on toilet for more than five seconds.	• Has stage fright. • Can't remember what to do here. • Needs emotional support.	• Hold a live demonstration. • Assist by unravelling entire toilet paper roll. • Sit on lap.
Human has somehow obtained fresh salmon/chicken and served on incorrect plate (theirs).	Human does not know difference between cat food and human food.	Yoink.

last words

In the coming weeks, months and years, your adopted human will carve out a place in your heart, and before long you'll completely forget what your world was like without them.

At times they will bother you, make too much noise, wake you up, rub you the wrong way, show no sympathy when you get spritzed by a rogue water bottle, and force you to seriously question all of the choices you made that led you to this existence.

Luckily, your short-term memory only lasts about 16 hours, so you can probably just take a decent nap and when you wake up everything will be fine. Your long-term memory will hold the grudges that really matter and put everything into perspective.

For each and every annoyance your human bestows upon you, they'll reward you tenfold with joy and love and delicious treats. Despite their many faults, humans can be pretty awesome creatures, and you have nine whole lives to spend shaping them into someone you can be truly proud of.

And hey, if you mess up, who cares? Nobody's gonna blame the cat.

Just try to find solace in the fact that even on your darkest days, when your human is driving you crazy and you feel like making a dash for that open door and returning to the wild ...

... your next catered meal is only a nap away.

In other words, going feral isn't worth the effort, bro.

acknowledgements

I'd like to say a humongous thanks to Alice, Tahlia, Nicci, Bonnee, Helen and the whole team at Hardie Grant Australia who, for some reason, thought the world needed more of my nonsense in it. Your support and guidance truly mean the world to me!

Thank you to my family: My heartbeats, Ciro and Seb, for being ridiculously supportive, loving and patient, and for always being by (and on) my side. Thank you to my sister, Britt, my bro-in-law, Chris, and my nephew, Reggie, for your unconditional love, unending support, and for letting me take over your house to write this. Thank you to my brother, Geoff, for having a face way dumber than mine. Oh, and I guess for all your help, support and ass-kicking, too.

Thank you Tash, Tam and Kate, for never ever giving up on me, and for helping me survive yet another truly ridiculous year! Yikes.

Thank you Alice M. for your vast knowledge and guidance.

Thank you to my hoes-fo-sho! Jess S (from conception to completion, whaaaaaat!!!!), Miranda, Vanessa, Cass, Rina, Hjords, Megan LK, Bec and Jess B. Thank you for being there both virtually and IRL, for encouraging me, for listening to me whinge, for giving me hugs and for just generally being awesome.

Everyone I've mentioned (and some I haven't), you're all the absolute greatest human beings to ever exist and I can't believe I get to know you in real life. Each and every one of you is truly chef's f**king kiss. No notes.

Ollie, it sucked all the balls to write this book without you by my side. I'm devastated you're not here, but I'm so grateful that you continue on this journey with me. You made all of this happen. I miss you every stupid damn freaking day.

Trim, thank you for stepping into Ollie's paw prints without missing a beat, and for being a true gentlecat about it. You're a sweetheart and a half, even though your meow is louder than a freight train and your butt has spent more time near my face than any butt ever should.

Mr Peanutbutter and BoJack, thank you for helping me convince all concerned parties that your adoption of me was in the interest of 'book research'. Looks like they fell for it. Suckers.

meet the author

Bexy McFly is an Australian-born writer, illustrator, graphic designer, animator and feline translator. Bexy has written several books, including *Cats Are The Worst!* and *Pussweek: A Cat's Guide to Feline Empowerment*, as well as the cult series *Pussweek | By Cats, For Cats*, an international publication she built from scratch (pun intended).

When she's not doing all the things, Bexy enjoys photographing stray food, staying out of the sun, cancelling social engagements, annihilating the patriarchy, putting on pyjamas and taking uninterrupted naps.

Published in 2025 by Hardie Grant Books, an imprint of Hardie Grant Publishing

Hardie Grant Books (Melbourne)
Wurundjeri Country
Level 11, 36 Wellington Street
Collingwood, Victoria 3066

Hardie Grant North America
2912 Telegraph Ave
Berkeley, California 94705

hardiegrant.com/books

Hardie Grant acknowledges the Traditional Owners of the Country on which we work, the Wurundjeri People of the Kulin Nation and the Gadigal People of the Eora Nation, and recognises their continuing connection to the land, waters and culture. We pay our respects to their Elders past and present.

All rights reserved. No part of this publication may be reproduced, stored in a retrieval system or transmitted in any form by any means, electronic, mechanical, photocopying, recording or otherwise, without the prior written permission of the publishers and copyright holders.

The moral rights of the author have been asserted.

Copyright text and illustration © Bexy McFly 2025
Copyright design © Hardie Grant Publishing 2025

A catalogue record for this book is available from the National Library of Australia

How to Adopt a Human
ISBN 978 1 76145 139 3

10 9 8 7 6 5 4 3 2 1

Publisher: Tahlia Anderson
Head of Editorial: Jasmin Chua
Project Editor: Nicci Dodanwela
Editor: Helen Koehne

Creative Director: Kristin Thomas
Designer: Bexy McFly
Head of Production: Todd Rechner

Colour reproduction by Splitting Image Colour Studio
Printed in China by Leo Paper Products LTD.

MIX
Paper | Supporting responsible forestry
www.fsc.org
FSC® C020056

The paper this book is printed on is from FSC®-certified forests and other sources. FSC® promotes environmentally responsible, socially beneficial and economically viable management of the world's forests.